NOTHING
SACRED
THE NEW CRICKET CULTURE

Edited by Alastair McLellan

TWO HEADS
PUBLISHING

CONTENTS

Introduction

WHOSE GAME IS IT ANYWAY?

'I am uneasy about the way he has a go at just about everything cricketers hold sacred.' This extract from Christopher Martin-Jenkins's review of Mike Marqusee's *Anyone But England* begs two questions: What are these things that cricketers are supposed to regard as 'sacred'? Why should any part of cricket be considered 'sacred' anyway? The answers to these two questions lie at the heart of the New Cricket Culture.

So what is the New Cricket Culture, who belongs to it and what does it hold 'sacred'. The answers to the first two questions can be found in this book's thirteen chapters. The answer to the third question, as you might have guessed, is 'nothing'.

That doesn't mean that the members of the NCC don't love cricket or that there aren't certain parts of the game – the five-day test match, leg-spin bowling – which they, along with the majority of cricket's more 'traditional' followers, believe are worth fighting hard to preserve.

But these things are not sacred. Cricket is a game, not a religion. Treating it as such, or at least imposing a set of (Victorian) values on it, is what has created cricket's image as an elitist sport, followed by people who abhor change and are therefore increasingly out of touch with the modern world around them.

Much was made of Test and County Cricket Board chairman Dennis Silk's outburst after England were knocked out of the

1996 World Cup. Here was a man, it was said, who would shake up the English game and get us winning again. And where did he place the blame for England's decline? On 'a degenerate nation that cannot be bothered to make an effort'. Directly criticising the real culprits, those that run the game, might have been a bit too close to home for an ex-public school headmaster and former president of the MCC. Yet again the cricket establishment reacted to a perceived crisis by telling the lower orders to pull their socks up.

Ever since cricket stopped simply being a way for sixteenth-century farmers to work up a thirst, too much of the English game has been about exclusion. If there is one thing that links the amateur/professional split and the MCC membership rules with the current ban on banners and musical instruments, reliance on credit-card booking for test match tickets and the Sky TV deal, it is the exclusion (directly or indirectly) of certain people from watching or playing the game. The NCC is, to employ a much-abused phrase, a broad church. In this book you'll find people who believe that the game's increased commercialism should be welcomed with open arms, treated as a necessary evil or opposed in all its forms. But one thing unites all members of the NCC – a desire to see cricket appeal to as many people as possible.

Not that we want this to happen simply out of the kindness of our hearts, you understand. Some of us are just fed up with going to the pub and finding that any discussion about cricket dries up after ten minutes because people would rather talk about football or music. We're sick of cricket being thought of as a sport followed by the reactionary or socially inadequate.

Late in 1995, 'Have I Got News For You' host Angus Deayton appeared on the BBC 2 programme 'Room 101'. The idea of the show was that guests would select the things they hated most and have them sent into obscurity via the doors of

'Room 101'. Deayton chose cricket.

When he announced his choice, the audience, mostly in their twenties and early thirties, let out a roar of approval. The cheers and laughs that greeted Deayton's selection were the kind produced when a really good, subtle observational joke hits home. Those in the audience sounded surprised by the amount of noise they had made, by how much they and those sitting around them obviously disliked cricket. But now that somebody like Deayton had voiced these feelings, they realised how strong they were. When 'Room 101' host and cricket fan Nick Hancock originally refused to consign the sport to the outer darkness, the audience yelled, stamped and clapped until he gave in.

I know it was only a bloody TV programme, but I still found it profoundly depressing.

So why did the audience react in that way? Is it, as some would suggest, because cricket is simply too boring to have any sort of mass appeal, that it lacks the drama, sophistication and excitement of, for example, Premier League football? That's obvious nonsense. Cricket was a mass spectator sport long before football, and in places like India and Sri Lanka it still is. As for the football comparison, anyone who has visited Lord's on a cup final day, the Sydney Cricket Ground during a day/night game, or Calcutta or Antigua for a test match will know that watching cricket can be as visceral an experience as any game of soccer.

Is it because 'young people today' simply lack the inclination or the attention span to want to watch cricket? More rubbish. Throughout the world, sports of all kinds are enjoying a massive surge in popularity. The reasons for this growth are cultural, commercial and political. They range from the UK's New Lad culture, to Rupert Murdoch's empire-building, to the nationalism of the Indian subcontinent. But whatever the inspiration, few major sports have struggled to expand their audience among the young. As for the attention-span argument, it's funny how often you here it side by side with comments about kids spending hours in front of their PCs picking their way through the Internet maze or tackling some fiendishly complex computer game.

The reason cricket too often evokes a dismissive reaction from the young, in the UK at least, is that it has become divorced from popular culture. Most UK sports lovers feel no affinity with the game, because little real attempt has been made to make cricket fit in to the way the majority of ordinary people live their lives in late-twentieth-century Britain. No sport thrives unless it reflects the lives and concerns of those who would support it given any encouragement.

Cricket has always been healthiest when it has been reacting to changes in the surrounding culture. During the last century, when cricket was establishing itself as England's national game, hardly a year went by without a major change in the way the game was played, administered or followed. The idea that cricket somehow embodies the values of an unchanging pre-industrial past is a profoundly misleading one. Cricket loves change.

And there's been change aplenty during the last ten years. A media revolution, the reintroduction of South Africa into test cricket, Sri Lanka rewriting cricket's world order, major tournaments announced in Canada, Singapore and Malaysia. But this tide of change seems to have passed English cricket by. All we've had so far is pathetic fiddling at the fringes, typified by the introduction of coloured clothing in the Sunday League. Does anybody imagine that this benefits the game in any way at all, apart from increasing the merchandising revenue of some counties.

What is needed now is real, fundamental change. How about

(for a start); a two-divisional championship to inject some life into the county game; significantly reduced entrance prices for mid-week county matches; a restriction on the reliance on credit-card booking for test match tickets; a better funded nationwide cricket development scheme; the introduction of a world test match championship to rival the World Cup as the focus of international cricket; a relaxation of the ridiculous rules that prohibit singing and waving banners at matches; and the imposition of limits on the number of seats allocated for corporate entertainment at major matches. And, hey! Why doesn't the TCCB fund a legal challenge to the European Court of Human Rights over the MCC's refusal to let women into the pavilion? Every little helps, and there's no doubt that this policy brings the game into disrepute.

The list goes on and on and on and on. It's not as if the game's administrators can claim poverty anymore. TV deals have made English cricket very rich. Let's see some of that money used in a constructive and coherent manner and not simply siphoned off to allow counties to upgrade their corporate entertainment facilities.

Cricket was part of English popular culture for over two hundred years and the NCC intends to drag it, kicking and screaming if necessary, away from those who want to limit its appeal.

Whose game is it anyway? That's for you to decide, and this book is here to help you make up your mind.

Welcome to the New Cricket Culture.

Alastair McLellan

THE WRITERS

DAVID COHEN is a feature writer for the *Independent*, *Guardian* and *GQ* magazine. Brought up in South Africa, Cohen qualified as a chartered accountant before commencing his career in journalism as a financial reporter with *Business Day*. He moved to England in 1987, where he read for a second degree in politics, philosophy and economics at Oxford University. After a spell as a City merchant banker with NM Rothschild & Sons, he returned to journalism in 1991. He captained his primary-school cricket team and once bowled six wides in one over – a school record which, he feels it is only right to report, still stands.

PHILLIP CORNWALL has supported Northamptonshire to three losing Lord's finals. In between disappointments, he works for football magazine *When Saturday Comes*, though he is truly terrible at both sports. He won third prize in the 1987 *Playfair Cricket Annual* quiz (£300 and two tickets to watch Northants throw away the NatWest Trophy. 'Still, it cleared the overdraft').

MATTHEW LOUKES is thirty one and remembers Mike Hendrick but not John Edrich. He was not educated in Eastbourne and lived for many years near the beautiful Saffrons Cricket Ground (the wall of which is very easy to climb). An early cricket coach described him as a talented rugby player, and warned that he should avoid cricket for fear of both injury and ridicule. He took vast amounts of Acid during the 1980s and became a bit of a rockin' hippy as a result with his body adornments and nipple attachments depicting the temple of Wu in a state of Karmic agitation. His rejuvenation as a cosmic spinner has not deflected his ardent passion for the works of Samuel Beckett and the live performances of Zandra from Denmark. He was an editorial board member of *Johnny Miller 96 Not Out* between 1993 and 1996.

IAN MACQUILLIN spent years saying he could produce a better magazine than the *Cricketer* and *Wisden Cricket Monthly*. He put his money where his mouth was when he launched *Third Man* in 1994. A journalist for eight years, Ian, who has worked for the *What Video* group and *Police Review*, is now deputy editor of a music industry trade paper, as well as being co-owner of small publisher The Publishing Collective, which produces specialist cricket magazine *Cricket Digest*. A lifelong cricket fan, Ian played first XI Surrey Championship cricket for Honor Oak and has also represented London Schools and Surrey Young Cricketers as an opening batsman.

MIKE MARQUSEE was born in New York City in 1953 and moved to Britain in 1971. He has worked as a youth worker, trade-union organiser, adult literacy tutor, sub-editor and journalist. A long-time political activist, he has supported more lost causes than he cares to remember – and has no regrets. He was editor of the left-wing *Labour Briefing*, a magazine reviled by Tony Blair's New Labour party. He is the author of *Slow Turn* (a thriller set on a cricket tour of India), *Defeat from the Jaws of Victory* (a critique of Neil Kinnock's leadership of the Labour Party) and *Anyone But England* (which was short-listed for the Sports Book of the Year award in 1994). His new book, *War Minus the Shooting*, is a personal account of the 1996 World Cup.

ALASTAIR MCLELLAN had a walk-on part in the *Sticky Wicket* and *Johnny Miller* stories. He also successfully killed off a third magazine by writing regularly for *Cricket Life International*.

He has written two controversial cricket books, *The Enemy Within?: The Impact of Overseas Players on English Cricket* and *Real Quick: A Celebration of the West Indian Pace Quartets* (with Michele Savidge). Neither outsold the Botham biography, but they both upset David Frith, so the author feels his job was well done. He now contributes to the New Cricket Culture standard-bearer, *Inside Edge*, while trying to find a publisher for his latest project, *Chris Tavare: Cricket's Cantona*.

IAN MCLELLAN is a graduate student at Lincoln College, Oxford who has just completed his doctoral thesis on seventeenth-century English prose romance. He has taught at the University of London for several years and his days are usually spent in the Duke Humfrey's room of Oxford's Bodleian library. He supports Kent cricket and spent much of the 1980s watching the team secure many spectacular victories (but no trophies) on glorious summer days, which, looking back, seem almost as unreal as a dream.

JIM MELLY is a writer, broadcaster and Mod, though probably not in that order. After a brief – and unspectacular – career as a pop star, he began writing on cricket, the media and political philosophy. He is currently working on turning his leg-break as far as his wrong 'un.

MICHELE SAVIDGE has been a sports journalist for fourteen years since joining the *Cricketer* in 1982. She then edited a number of sports and fitness magazines before returning to the cricket world as deputy editor of Imran Khan's *Cricket Life International* magazine. In 1991, she became the first female sports sub-editor on the *London Evening Standard*. With Alastair McLellan, she is co-author of *Real Quick: A Celebration of the West Indian Pace Quartets*. She is now a freelance writer, living in London but pining after her spiritual home in Antigua.

MARTIN SPEIGHT is a flamboyant cricketer and a talented artist. He attended Hurstpierpoint College and Durham University. He has represented Sussex at all levels, making his first XI debut in 1986. Having missed most of the 1995 season with post-viral fatigue syndrome, he is now back to full fitness and wowing the Hove faithful with his extravagant reverse sweep.

FRANCIS WHEEN writes columns for the *Guardian*, *Esquire* and *Private Eye* and is a panelist on Radio 4's 'News Quiz' and BBC TV's 'Late Review'. His books include *The Sixties*, *Television* and *Tom Driberg: His Life and Indiscretions*. An occasional wicket-keeper and belatedly improving batsman, he plays cricket for his village side in Essex and for a team of local farmers. In another life, he hopes to come back as Nasser Hussain.

A CRICKET NIGHTMARE

1

NOTES FROM THE UNDERGROUND
Mike Marqusee

Cricket books are full of lies. I used to read them, a long time ago, before I found out the truth.

I got the books from my brother. He was a scavenger until they sent him to a Detention Zone. He hated cricket; Total-box was his thing. But when he came across old cricket books in the course of his work, he always gave them to me.

'Here, little sister,' he used to growl. 'You're the only one who wants this worthless crap.' True enough. If he could've sold them, even for a single nourishment credit, he would have. That's the way he was.

I'm thinking about him a lot these days, now that I'm in a Zone myself. It was the graffiti that got me Zoned, but it's the lies in the books and the digi-casts that I can't get out of my head. At our trial the socio-lawyers talked a load of rubbish about 'underground cricket' and where it came from, why we played it, who we are. Not that any of it mattered when the judge sentenced us.

'You are parasites!' the old git crowed. 'You are a menace to decent people. You have no respect for the game of cricket or for the fundamental principles of intellectual property enshrined in GATT VII.'

Well, I plead guilty to the last charge and nothing I've seen or heard in the Zone has rehabbed me yet.

One of the few useful things I ever learned from a cricket book was the fact that a long time ago the game didn't belong to anyone. You didn't need a licence to play. There was a time when nobody had heard of either GladCric International or MCCGetty PLC. Not many people nowadays know it, but there was even a time when you could watch the digi-casts of big matches for free. All that was before what came to be known as the great fissure, when world cricket split into two.

When I was a kid everyone in my estate was into virtual and interactive cricket. We used to think it was brilliant: getting live-wired so you could play against the famous gladiators, going ape when you took a wicket or hit a ten. My brother used to laugh at me as I stood in the kitchen, the hyper-reality visor clamped down over my face, flinging my arms up in the air and shouting 'Howzzatttt!'

He thought the gladiators were a bunch of wankers. I used to get angry with him for spoiling my fun. Man, I was a GladCric fanatic in those days. I never missed a digi-cast. So much happened on the multi-screen, so many emotional ups and downs, so many titanic feats. The two hours felt like a lifetime. I used to walk around our estate in a pair of Glad-goggles. Of course they weren't the real sphere-enhancing optics the gladiators themselves wore. Only the kids in the gated communities could afford those. But they looked like the real thing and they made me feel dead cool.

More than anything I wanted to go to one of the arenas to watch the gladiators play live. A friend of mine got in once. She told me it was like sitting in this huge crystal with all these silicon facets filled with giant images. She said it was even better than the digi-casts because the whistle of the sphere as it flew across the playing core was so loud it made your ears ring for days after. And the multi-coloured laser trail it left in the air was so intense it flashed up in front of your eyes even when you closed them hours later. One weird thing, though, was that the music you heard on the digi-casts was dubbed in later on. You got the non-stop verbals, but they didn't quite sound the same without the heavy synths. It made the breaks between the overs feel strangely empty. She also told me Savage II looked much smaller in the crystal than on the digi-cast and that Blitzkrieg's long blond wig fell off when he dived across the crease trying to sneak a quick single.

In those days I thought she was incredibly lucky to get to see GladCric live. Tickets for GladCric were booked years in advance and cost a fortune. Most spectators could only afford to go if they bought a winning lotto ticket, so I used to spend every spare nourishment credit I had on the lotto. Now I realise she wasn't lucky. None of us were lucky. They should have paid us to go. The spectators were as much a part of the spectacle as the gladiators themselves. My friend told me how they flashed up prompts for the fans on the giant VDUs. 'Freak out!' one unit would say. 'What a load of rubbish!' another would shout. Each bank of spectators in each facet would follow its allocated prompter. They told you when and what to shout. 'Louder! Louder!' they commanded, and all those morons did as they were told, shouting themselves hoarse. It was all for the digi-casts. Everything was for the digi-casts.

Someone I met in the Zone told me about a Perpetual World Cup match between Neebox-Rike and Mega-Card. Apparently, the entire computer program went down. Suddenly there were no non-stop verbals and no one to tell you what was happening in front of your eyes. The giant simul-screens and instant replays went blank, and the fan prompters dissolved into abstract patterns like mysterious hieroglyphs. At first everyone was confused. The gladiators looked so tiny and far away. They kept playing, it seems that inside their helmets they were still receiving the game script, but they looked bloody silly without all the techno-enhancement. The cheerleaders kept prancing around the edges of the playing core but you couldn't hear them, and from such a vast distance they looked even sillier than the gladiators. People started talking among themselves, asking the fans around them what they thought was happening in the game and analysing it together. Some people began imitating the non-stop verbals and even taking the piss out of the compu-commentators' accents.

I suppose if it had spread, if we could have sabotaged the compu-commentators and the fan prompts, we could have reclaimed the game. But the security at GladCric was always intense. Everyone was screened three times before entering the crystal and you couldn't even get a ticket if your name wasn't on the EuroPol safe list.

The big corps used to send scouts to our estate to recruit talent for their cricket academies. One of my brother's mates even got a trial with McMicrosoft. But if you didn't make it, got into trouble with unapproved drugs or injured yourself, the big corps threw you back to the estates like the broken bats the kids from the gated communities discarded, which the scavengers used to sell us in exchange for nicotine vouchers.

Everyone used to say that the best thing that could happen to you was getting scouted by one of the talent trawlers for Heritage Cricket. The money was even better than for GladCric. I had only ever seen the edited highlights of Heritage Cricket, available on the 444-channel Skycard. If you wanted to see the whole five-day match live, with all the action and the ritual digi-cast as it happened at Lord's, you had to have the 2222-channel Skycard, and even some of the kids in the gated communities couldn't afford that. I was always intrigued by the glimpses of Heritage Cricket I did get to see, though I couldn't understand all the rules and rigmarole. For a start, both teams played in white. How could fans tell them apart?

I used to fantasise about wearing those gleaming white outfits and playing Heritage Cricket, but of course I was a girl and one of the reasons for the great fissure was that the big corps wanted women to play so that they could have a wider and more varied spread of product promotion. Everyone knew about Lord's' great tradition of not letting women into the pavilion. So I was doomed, even if I hadn't been a mongrel without a hope in hell of passing the Henderson Test, an absolute prerequisite for getting into the Heritage Cricket academies, which were strictly segregated according to national type.

I met a bloke in the Zone who said he had attended one of the GladCric academies before he got chucked out for disobeying the script. He confirmed what most of us had long believed: GladCric was rigged. The big corps worked out everything on the basis of computer analyses of spectator preferences, combined with complex trade-offs among their various global and regional commercial interests. It all depended on which products they were trying to sell to whom at any given point in the Perpetual World Cup. I suppose we knew this all along. Back on the estate everyone used to gossip about which one of the gladiators had been bribed by the other side to throw away his wicket or drop a catch. That was part of the fun.

In any case, nowadays the big profits don't come from the matches or the digi-casts but from the virtual and interactive gladiator spin-offs that people play at home and in the cyber-cafes. Few could afford to go to the matches and the punishment for playing unlicensed cricket could be severe, so all you had left was live-wiring. A lot of us got so hooked on it we couldn't tell the difference between virtual GladCric and the real thing. There were hundreds of virtual cricket leagues and knock-out comps. And when I was little every estate used to have its own cyber-tournaments. I used to beat my brother's mates regularly, which pissed them off but gave him a buzz. "I still think it's a wanker's game," he said with a smile, before going off to practise drop-kicks for Total-box.

Then about ten years ago they launched the comprehensive info-privatisations and after that the big piracy crackdown. The new programs were coded with EuroPol digital locks so almost no one on the estates could get access to them any more. Pretty soon all the live-wiring was obsolescent and you couldn't even dump it on a scavenger. That was when we finally started playing cricket. Not the virtual version but the real thing, or at least as close to the real thing as we could get in the underground garages, blind alleys and elevated walkways. We changed the rules to fit the circumstances. We cobbled together bats and balls out of bits and pieces the scavengers sold us. One day my brother came home with a bat made out of wood. I think it might even have been willow. I'd never seen a willow bat before, but I had read about them in a book once. The bat was nearly split in half, but I still thought it was beautiful. I was amazed when he gave it to me for nothing. All he'd ever given me before were things like books that he couldn't flog to anyone at any price. I loved that bat. I spent hours repairing it with glue and tape and then I painted it bright orange and wrote my name on it in big black letters. My brother told me I was a clot-head, but I think he was secretly pleased.

Of course we didn't have the laser beam stumps they have in GladCric, and even if we could have afforded the wooden stumps they have in Heritage Cricket there was no way we could get them to stand up on concrete. So we took to spray-painting the three stumps on brick and cement walls. And that was how we got our nickname. That was how the Stumpie Posse came into being.

Now I've heard an awful lot of bollocks on the digi-caster about the "stumpie conspiracy" and how spraying the sign of the stumps in public places is a cry of anguish from a dispossessed underclass. So I want to use these notes to set the record straight.

First of all, there's no "conspiracy". The hawks like to think that there is because then they can round us all up and frogmarch us through the courts and into the Zones. But I can tell you I'd never even met the other stumpies I was tried with until the morning they put us together in the dock. Later in the cells and now in the Zone, we've talked a lot. We all got into playing 'underground' cricket more or less the same way. Some of the younger kids never even played the virtual stuff, but they saw their older brothers and sisters playing the real game and joined in. As for the sign of the stumps, it started spontaneously about the same time on different estates. We sprayed our three stumps wherever we had to. Sure, it was a dead give-away to the GATT-cops. They could tell someone was playing unlicensed cricket as soon as they saw those tell-tale marks, and those bastards always want to make someone pay, guilty or innocent. And since you could get nicked whether or not you touched a cricket bat, there was no reason not to go on with the game. Part of the fun was doing it in secret, getting away with it under the GATT-cops' noses and making fools of their informers on the estates. Pretty soon we sprayed the sign of the stumps everywhere we could, even if we weren't playing cricket, just to set a false trail for the GATT-cops.

In a society where even failure to report unapproved graffiti can get you Zoned, the sudden appearance of the sign of the stumps throughout cities and suburbs, even on the security perimeters of the gated communities and the military-financial precincts, caused quite a stir. Rival theories filled the inter-news columns and Net-channels, though they mostly kept it off the digi-casts for fear of sparking "copy-cat" activity. Some attributed the stumpie phenomenon to the corrupting influence of GladCric. The experts had a field-day. Some of them even claimed it was just a pointless craze. They said we didn't even know the sign had anything to do with cricket.

Basically, to begin with, we made the sign of the stumps so we could play cricket and get away with playing cricket. Then we just liked it, because we liked the game it stood for, so we started putting it up everywhere. And the more it annoyed people, the more we wanted to do it. As for the stumpie thing being 'a cry of anguish from a dispossessed underclass', the doves missed the whole point, as usual. We didn't play cricket to get back at the spoiled bastards in the gated communities. We played cricket because it was fun. We would suss out a place to play, anywhere away from the GATT-cops and the grasses would do as long as it had a few yards of hard, flat surface against which we could bounce whatever sphere came to hand.

We played some epic games, late into the night, with batsmen mounting brilliant rearguard defensive innings and bowlers tormenting them with over after over of cunning accuracy. We had fielders who could snap up a ricochet off a garage ceiling and turn and hit the spray-on stumps in the blink of an eye. Pretty soon rumours spread about the best players and we were challenged by a neighbouring estate to a match in an abandoned warehouse in a no-go precinct. It went on for four days and nights. We kept our twelfth men posted outside to keep watch for the GATT-cops. Some grass came by and we had to beat him up, but aside from that we played without interruption. I scored a century in five and a half hours. It took a lot of concentration because under the warehouse rules the most you could score off any single stroke was two.

After we won that match a couple of us went totally crazy and got ourselves tattooed with the sign of the stumps. Just a small tattoo, hard to read if you didn't get up close or know what you were looking for, but it meant something to us. It gave me a kick to walk past a GATT-cop and smile at him, my mother taught me always to smile at cops, and know he couldn't see my tattoo concealed under my clothes. My brother told me I was daft. Later, when they busted me at Lord's, threw me naked into a cell and gave me a special kicking because of the tattoo, I realised he was right.

It was shortly after my brother got Zoned for killing a man in an unlicensed Total-box match (the promoter bribed the cops and walked free, so someone had to take the rap) that I decided to make my perverse pilgrimage to Lord's.

Despite what they said in court, there was no master plan to disrupt Heritage Cricket. EuroPol made a big deal at our trial about the high tech. sleuthing that had enabled them to capture the "terrorists". That was just more bullshit, it all happened by accident.

At the labour market they were signing up catering workers for the annual Gentlemen v. Players Match at Lord's. I applied, thinking I'd never get past the security screen, but they must've been desperate because after two weeks I got an e-mail notice telling me where and when to report for work.

I can't tell you exactly when I got the idea, but by the time I reported to the precinct depot I knew exactly what I wanted to do. The sign of the stumps was glowing in my brain like a prompt on one of the giant VDUs at the GladCric match. Even then I thought I would probably be screened out after the coach crossed the inner line, but I was determined to get as far as I could.

The prosecutors thought I must have had inside help but it isn't true. People like me learn how to pass unnoticed when we want to, when we have to. We know how to blend in with the crowd.

From the books my brother gave me I learned that for two

hundred years Lord's had stood in a place called St John's Wood in the middle of London. They only moved it into the country after the third wave of urban riots left most of the area a charred no-go precinct.

Of course, everyone these days sees Lord's as the epitome of the restricted-access countryside. After all, it's one of Europe's top elite theme parks. As our coach passed through the security perimeter (I kept my eyes blank as the Group Four storm troopers boarded the vehicle) I felt a surge of excitement. This would be real cricket at last, not that GladCric fakery. This would be the beautiful game I'd glimpsed on the digi-caster and read about in books. The giant sign over the gateway seemed to confirm these hopes: 'Heritage Cricket, the true contest'.

They assigned us to bunks in the staff hostel, carefully hidden from view on the edge of the park. We were the usual mix: catering workers, cleaners, prostitutes. Most were migrants and they spoke a babble of languages. They stuck us all in Lord's uniforms (for which we all had to deposit our global PIN codes).

When I first glimpsed cricket at Lord's, I came close to abandoning all my secret plans. It was such a luxury; like some of the food we served the spectators, I kept wanting to nibble at it when no one was watching.

My first view of a turf wicket and a green outfield with white-clad figures moving gracefully across it took my breath away. Amazingly, there were no sponsors' logos anywhere, not even on the players' clothing. From books I knew that the brick and iron-work pavilion was an exact replica of the one that had graced the old St John's Wood ground, though I soon found that, contrary to myth, women were admitted within its hallowed walls – someone had to wash the dishes and clean the toilets.

GladCric is played in giant self-enclosed geodesic structures, but Heritage Cricket at Lord's is open to the sky. I never realised what a soaring feeling of limitless space that gives you. Of course, a plastic luminescent dome springs into place if the weather turns ugly. These people pay a lot of money for a week or two at the theme park and they expect to see cricket – rain or shine.

How strange it was to see the game played without helmets, shoulder pads or torso armour. And instead of the gladiators' electro-sensitive body-fitted prosthetic extensions the batsmen wore these awkward looking bulky, springy gloves; instead of slimline flexi-guards they wore floppy pads on their legs. The first morning, after the Gentlemen had won the toss (apparently they always win the toss) and the openers had marched into bat, I have to admit I froze in my place for a second, completely entranced by the spectacle. Then some silly bastard in one of these orange and yellow ties started bawling for service and I had to hop to it. From that moment on I remembered to pretend that people like me had no business watching Heritage Cricket.

But as I scurried about my duties I kept half an eye on the action on the pitch. They use a red ball covered with leather, with a big fat seam protruding around its circumference. It doesn't travel nearly as fast as the translucent GladCric laser-gyroscopic spheres but I was amazed at what some of the bowlers could do with it, just by a flick of the wrist. The batsmen stroked the ball so that, more often than not, it rolled along the grass. I hadn't realised how lovely that could be. Words and phrases I'd read in old cricket books came back to me...cover drive, leg glance, soft hands...

About half way through the first session of play I saw one of the rituals for which Lord's is famous. In Heritage Cricket they have real live umpires, one standing behind the stumps at the bowler's end and the other at square leg. At a certain, predetermined moment in the game the umpires 'get it wrong'. This was very popular and always included in the digi-cast highlights. Of course, just like in GladCric, all the decisions were really made by a computer network of electronic eyes.

The umpires were linked to the network by ear-pellets and simply carried out the computer's adjudications. I have to admit that it did make the game seem more human. I guess that's why they evolved the ritual of 'getting it wrong', to make the illusion of humanness more convincing. At a certain point, the computer was programed to misinform the umpires so that they 'got it wrong'. I noticed that when this happened (two or three times a day) all the box-dwellers fell about in fits of self-satisfied laughter.

The few days I spent working at Lord's were a revelation. Sometimes there seemed to be more ritual than cricket. All the cricketers clapped the opposition at the least excuse. If any of the gladiators had done that they would have had their heads split open, if not by team-mates then by spectators. But Heritage Cricket was different: there was "inspecting the wicket", "taking the new ball", "drinks" and "tea". The wooden stumps rattled when they were hit by a ball instead of sounding a siren like in GladCric.

There were digi-cameras everywhere, just as many as at GladCric, but they were carefully concealed, operated from an info-site suspended high above the ground and obscured from the boxes. They don't have the giant VDUs and crystal facets you get at GladCric, but each box is equipped with an array of multi-screens for private use. And you can program your own preferred commentary on the match and listen to it on ear-pellets. You can mix and match the voices of any and all of the greats, Johnners, Arlott, Aggers, Athers and of course those two old-fashioned warhorses, Fred Trueman and Phil Tufnell. You can surf from one voice to another or even synth conversa-

tions between them. I noticed that in some boxes famous cricketers of the past were at the service of the spectators, telling
stories or pouring drinks. Apparently, when you sign up with
Heritage Cricket it's a lifetime contract. In the evenings the
players, present as well as past, mingled with the theme park
guests (and, according to the gossip in the hostel, sexually
serviced them, male and female alike).

The cricketers all had these old-fashioned names and the
miniaturised scoreboards in each box referred to them by their
initials. For some reason, the Gentlemen had their initials
before, and the Players after, their surnames. Because I had read
those books my brother gave me, I realised that these names
were not the players' real names. They were assigned to them
by the organisers, just like the names in GladCric. There was
Bradman, Hobbs, Hutton, O'Reilly, Larwood, Sobers,
Richards, Gower, Botham.... There was even a bloke in a long
beard called Grace. Of course, some names are forbidden,
Greig, Malcolm, Lara, players of the past who had brought the
true heritage of cricket into disgrace.

As I wandered from box to box, I realised that not many of
the box-dwellers actually watched the cricket. Quite a few were
snoozing with their ear-pellets turned to the ambient music
channel. Others were freebasing coke and talking about money
and politics. Behind the rows of boxes (each with a brass plate
denoting the name of the big corp that owned it) the ground
was honeycombed with meeting rooms and info-tech centres.
Our supervisors told us to keep sharp; this was one of the
premier matches of the year at Lord's and important deals
would be struck by the box-dwellers in the coming days. One
of these cringing creeps even informed us in awed tones that the
last two World Bank presidents had been chosen here during
the luncheon interval.

In keeping with ancient tradition, the MCC committee

always included at least one former Prime Minister and one EU commissioner. Of course, the committee's functions these days were purely honorary. All the shares in the company that owned it, and indeed the rights to Heritage cricket worldwide, were controlled by J. Paul Getty VII, who was not a biological descendant of the great patron, but the chairman of the MCC holding corporation, who assumed the name by right, just as Kerry Packer IX did when taking the helm at GladCric International.

Outside the Lord's gates, at the end of the day's play, a queue of desperate-looking men in shabby clothes and trainers with holes in them waited patiently to pick up the litter left by the box-dwellers. Needless to say, they were actors. The real homeless and unemployed were all confined to indigent camps hundreds of kilometres from Lord's or else were serving in work-fare regiments reclaiming polluted ex-industrial wasteland. The actors were hired to portray this scene from the late twentieth century because the box-dwellers enjoyed gawping and laughing and shouting abuse at the poor. After all, they'd paid for the Heritage experience and they had a right to the whole shebang.

Seeing them smirk and listening to their belly-laughs made me remember why I had come.

Late one night I crept out of the hostel and took the service lift to the walkways that surmounted the highest tier of boxes. The view across the theme park was tremendous. I could see the arcade leading to the Grace Gates, lined by statues of the great figures of the past: Thomas Lord, Lord Harris, Sir Pelham Warner, E.W. Swanton, Rupert Murdoch. I could see the rose gardens and the marquees, the guest bungalows and night-clubs, the golf courses and nature trails, and in the distance the twinkling lights atop the security fences.

Then suddenly I remembered something I had read in a book.

'Where's Father Time?' I wondered, and I must have wondered it aloud, because a voice came from behind me, 'Buried in a vault somewhere. There's no memento mori allowed here.'

I whirled around, shocked but ready to take whatever action was necessary to defend myself, only to be confronted by a smiling old man in an info-tech worker's uniform.

'How on earth did you know about Father Time?' he asked

'Books', I said. 'My brother was a scavenger.'

'So not all of you have been corrupted by GladCric then?'

'I know about Father Time and much more.' And to prove my point I rattled off the names of the great players who had graced Lord's in the past and the great feats it had witnessed. The old man shook his head. 'That was a different Lord's, a different game. No one plays real cricket anymore.'

'I do,' I insisted boldly. 'My friends do. We play real cricket all the time.'

At first he seemed frightened by this confession, then intrigued.

'You play cricket? Without a licence?'

'Sure, why not?' I was feeling bold or possibly just crazy from the tranquillizers the supervisors gave us after we finished the day's work. 'I can turn an off-break two feet on a solid concrete surface,' I boasted.

'You're one of them,' he said. 'What do they call them? Stumpers?'

'Stumpies,' I pronounced with pride.

'And you really play real cricket? I mean you don't know the result in advance? Every player plays under the same rules?'

'Of course. That's the fun of it. We're not into that GladCric bullshit.'

He beckoned me to follow him and together we climbed up a steel ladder into what I immediately realised was the central info-site for the ground. He explained that many decades ago he had attended one of the academies and showed much promise as a middle-order batsman. Many times he had thought of leaving the game, but he had been employed by Heritage Cricket too long and was afraid of life outside. What would there be for him, at his age? Life as a migrant or, worse yet, an indigent? Many years before he had come from an estate like mine, but he didn't know where his family was today or if any of them were still alive. The info-site at Lord's was his only home.

'Besides, it's an IT classified level-four job. If I violated the access restrictions they'd Zone me immediately.' He pointed to the blue patch on his wrist, where the semi-conductor had been implanted.

I asked him what they taught at the academy. 'Oh it's all different now. These days they mainly do media studies, drama, accents, commerce awareness.'

'And cricket?'

'Yes, some cricket. But most of it's choreographed in advance, by this little genius', he patted the bank of VDUs and keypads as if it was a favourite nephew, 'after all, we have to make sure the Gentlemen win. Even if all the Gentlemen are really Players pretending to be Gentlemen.'

I must have looked startled because he smiled and explained, 'The customer is always right. He who pays the piper calls the tune.'

'But what about the "true contest"?'

'People believe what they want to believe.'

'And the Ashes matches?' I asked. 'Okay, the box-dwellers like the Gentlemen to win but what about "England" and "Australia"?'

'Funny how people love the old names even when the real things vanished years ago,' he mused. 'See, this is how we do it.'

And he showed me on one of the VDUs how they manipulated the imagery, and the result. 'We change the scores depending on where the match is being digi-cast. All the box-dwellers are booked in advance here and their preferences tabulated so most of them get to see what pleases them. Watch: "England" is winning here, but over here,' and he took me to another VDU, 'where the satellite has a Pacific footprint, "Australia" is winning'.

I must have looked shocked.

'You think the rich are any different from the people who like GladCric?' he smiled at my innocence. 'They like to have their cake and eat it too, even more than the rest of us, because they're addicted to it. It's their daily diet.'

Having served the box-dwellers over the last few days, I knew what he meant.

'Was it always like this?' I asked, suddenly alarmed that all those old books, the videos, the CDs were nothing but lies, that there had never been a 'true contest'.

He searched his memory. 'No, I don't think so. I don't think it was that way when I started out. I think the scores were the same everywhere. I think the players didn't know what was going to happen before they started playing. But maybe I was kidding myself.'

'It must have changed when they had the great fissure.'

'Great carve-up, you mean,' he snorted, 'great con-job.'

He looked at me with disappointment, as if he had expected more of me. 'I thought you knew about cricket! There was no great fissure. It's all the same people. The same people it always was and always will be.'

'I don't understand.'

'MCCGetty PLC and GladCric International are both subsidiaries of the same company. Look around. Haven't you seen the names on the brass plates on the boxes? Can't you see they're the same as the names of the gladiator teams in the Perpetual World Cup? Haven't you figured it out yourself? J. Paul Getty VII and Kerry Packer IX are one and the same.'

We talked about many things late into the night, and much that hadn't made sense to me before became clear. I was back in the hostel pretending to be asleep when the dawn broke, but it didn't take them long to arrest me. Maybe the old man grassed me up, but I doubt it. The hostels are full of sneaks and snitches, and someone must have noticed me slip out and in. After that, it must have been easy to link me to the huge sign of the stumps spray-painted on the sightscreen at the Nursery End, where every box-dwelling scumbag could see it.

Even in the Zone, we've found some places to play cricket, though they send us to the punishment block whenever they catch us. We've got nothing to draw stumps with here, no spray paint, not even any chalk (too many compulsive graffitists here to allow that), so we've started building wickets out of broken bricks. Sometimes I remember my brother and the bat he gave me and those all-night games we played in the underground garage where the ball would ricochet off the ceiling and you could be caught out off the top of your head. I think of those games and I know that the 'true contest' will always and only belong to us.

THE NEW CRICKET CULTURE

2

WHO'S AFRAID OF THE BARMY ARMY
Ian MacQuillin

Ian Wooldridge, the *Daily Mail's* cricket correspondent, would like to see Alison and Charlie Mellor dead. His preferred method of execution, chosen by the award-winning journalist during England's Ashes tour of 1994–5, is the gas chamber.

In the eyes of Wooldridge and many of his peers, the Mellors' crime was a serious one. You see, at tests and one-day internationals that winter, Alison and Charlie Mellor wore T-shirts with Union Jacks on them and sang, chanted and supported in a manner more in keeping with a soccer international than the gentlemanly endeavour of an Ashes series.

Wooldridge's wrath knew no bounds. To him, Alison and Charlie Mellor, and their colleagues in what came to be known on that tour as the Barmy Army, were 'soccer hooligans', 'confrontational morons' and 'the detritus of the British national social system'. Referring to a conversation with Graham Halbish, chief executive of the Australian Cricket Board, in which Halbish was reported to have said that he would like to see the Barmy Army gassed, Wooldridge wrote: 'It is a wholly politically incorrect remark and I support him.'

The one flaw in Wooldridge's otherwise faultless and cogently argued case is that the Mellors are neither 'morons', or 'hooligans'. Both, in fact, are constables in the Metropolitan Police. Alison is a graduate entrant nearing the end of a three-

37

year posting to a south London child-protection team. The Mellors are, in fact, the type of people the *Daily Mail* in normal circumstances regards as pillars of British society. Yet all this has counted for nothing. They were demonised by the press and the cricket establishment simply because of the manner in which they follow the England team.

Alison and Charlie Mellor are not isolated examples of the way cricket is being supported in the middle of the 1990s. It is a little premature to talk of a coherent movement, but it is perfectly fair and accurate to say that a distinct New Cricket Culture has developed over the past few years and is still developing now. And far from being the scum of the earth and a major threat to the bedrock of Western civilisation that we all know cricket to be (God, after all, is an Englishman – or at least born in southern Africa but England qualified), it is patently obvious to anyone with half a brain that this new breed of cricket fan holds the key to the regeneration of the game.

The arithmetic is very simple. The game has been in a steady, if not terminal, decline as its fan base has narrowed. The *Cricketer's* circulation is declining, for example, because its subscribers are dying. The game desperately needs an influx of younger fans. That much is obvious. It also needs more money. The Test and County Cricket Board believed that these two birds could be killed with the one stone: it signed a deal with BSkyB, which was willing to pay well for cricket (£58 million for a four-year deal), and which employed a marketing approach that was guaranteed to appeal to a younger audience.

Unfortunately for the cricket authorities, the quest for the hearts and minds of the younger generation has coincided with the cultural empowerment of youngish men and women who, while liberal and intelligent, aren't ashamed to admit that they enjoy shagging and getting pissed. But worse than this, much worse, is that they have no inherent respect for the establishment. Cricket has imported a load of New Lads (and some Laddesses) and now has no earthly idea what to do about them.

The origin of New Laddism and its debt to football culture is documented elsewhere in this book. It is sufficient to realise that the New Cricket Culture is not only a product of cricket itself, but a byproduct of the sociological New Lad phenomenon as expressed by magazines such as *Loaded* and football programmes such as 'Fantasy Football League', however, cricket's New Lads do have their own distinct profile.

The most obvious example of cricketing Laddism is the appearance of the Barmy Army and other football-style fans at cricket grounds. But there is a clear distinction between the original cadre of Barmy Army troopers who coalesced spontaneously during the 1994–5 Ashes series and any old Union flag-waving fan at a cricket match – something the cricket press cannot, or will not, recognise. The Barmy Army were a real entity based on the tour-generated camaraderie of genuine cricket fanatics: after all, what other word would you use to describe people who take six-weeks unpaid leave or spend their redundancy money travelling halfway round the world to watch England get stuffed out of sight. What the cricket press, and we can presume the cricket authorities, failed or chose not to comprehend was that these hard-core fans were not louts who had no appreciation of the finer points of the game. They cared deeply. That's why they were there.

The football-style supporting tactics of the original Barmy Army and their subsequent imitators around the test-match grounds in 1995 were based on nothing less than adulation for the likes of Darren Gough, Mike Atherton and Dominic Cork. When they did well, the crowd got behind them like no other cricket crowd has inspired and lifted a cricketer since Ian Botham's comeback against New Zealand at the Oval in 1986 when he overhauled Dennis Lillee's record for the number of test wickets. (At that game, the atmosphere was so thick and tangible, it seemed to charge the ions being emitted by my TV set.) Darren Gough and Phil DeFreitas's ultimately match-winning stand against South Africa at the Oval in 1994 or Dominic Cork's Old Trafford hat trick the following year are other excellent and obvious examples. And the post-Adelaide Test party in January 1995 is legendary (at least in Barmy Army circles) for the egalitarian mixing of test player, fan and booze. When England do not do well, the Barmy Army, in traditional British fashion, uncorks a 1940 vintage bottle of Chateau Dunkirk, launches into a chorus of 'Always Look on the Bright Side of Life', and offers up unquestioning devotion to the forlorn English hope.

Back in England for the 1995 West Indies series, riding on the publicity created by the Barmy Army the previous winter, it was much easier to notice the English fans who supported the game in much the same way. (The original Barmy Army, now transformed into a business, turned out only for the severely truncated Saturday of the Edgbaston test.) Stands such as the Western Terrace at Headingley, or the Scoreboard End at Trent Bridge are noisy and raucous. They can also be home to highly witty souls and being among them can be damn good fun.

Many of them though, are not die-hard cricket fans. Many are not really cricket fans at all. Their one day at a test match (usually Saturday) will probably be the only game of cricket, professional or otherwise, they see all year. Yet among the groups of robed Elvises (Trent Bridge 1995), nuns with suspiciously hairy legs (Headingley 1995) and bewigged, false-moustached Brookside Scallies (everywhere except Lord's and the Oval) there is almost invariably at least one cricket anorak. During the research to assess the level of cricketing knowledge of test crowds I helped carry out in 1995, most of these groups of 'football supporters' scored highly in a questionnaire that asked questions such as 'Who is currently top of the county Championship?', 'Name one of the ICC Associate Members taking part in the World Cup?', 'Who has recorded the best test innings bowling figures?' and 'Who topped the first-class batting averages in 1994?'. In fact, if your life depended on the answers given by a group of herberts in fancy dress or a single county member in a Panama hat munching on his chicken drumsticks, the lads would be far more likely to keep the electric chair at bay.

As has been said, the press, for reasons best known to themselves, prefer to consider cricket's New Lads as nothing more than football supporters who have forgotten that the soccer season is over. But they are just one facet of the New Cricket Culture. The other branch, which has received little publicity, is poorly known and has been virtually ignored by the press, has the makings of an intellectual movement. This sounds a grand, almost arrogant claim. But it is the truth nonetheless, and it is from among these fans that cricket's new intelligentsia is coalescing.

Forget the flag-waving velcro-headed Scallies, the New Cricket Culture is forming now among young, intelligent, questioning people who have a passion for cricket and are independently developing similar opinions about the game. This is what defines the movement. There are no youth tribes associated with cricket as there are in football. Music does not play such an important part in cricket; neither does fashion. Whatever happens in the outside world, it is unlikely you well ever see cricket casuals at a test match. What you have though, are tens of thousands of people aged around eighteen to thirty-five who have looked at the dog's dinner that passes for English cricket in the 1990s and come up with the same conclusions.

Typical new generation cricket followers believe there should be a two-divisional championship. They think the England team should be managed by a player recently retired from, or even still playing, first-class cricket. Ian Botham or Allan Lamb are the names most would have given in 1995. By and large, they are not fans of Ray Illingworth and think he has been a total git to Mike Atherton, though it should be said they liked Ted Dexter considerably less. They are big, big fans of certain players, so much so that these players can hardly do anything wrong. The big three are Mike Atherton, Dominic Cork and Darren Gough, ably supported by Alec Stewart and Graham Thorpe. Angus Fraser is up there too, as is Jack Russell. The jury is still out on Graeme Hick and Mark Ramprakash (but it has returned a verdict on Peter Martin, inspired by the 'wanker' sign he gave to Barmy Army supporters in South Africa). If you think Mike Atherton should be England captain, you are part of the New Cricket Culture. If you think it should be Dermot Reeve, your heart's in the right place but you're not really on the same wavelength. If you think that grammar-school upstart Atherton should have been sacked months ago and Mark Nicholas brought out of retirement, you are clearly a Nazi.

The new generation, though hardly fans of Mr Murdoch's attempts at creating a global media empire, are supporters of Sky's cricket coverage. They applaud the way it has brought to the screen cricket that would have gone unbroadcast if left to the BBC. Mind you they'd also say Charles Colvile is a prat and Richie Benaud has golden bollocks. Many of the NCC members play the game at club level, some are quite good. But a surprisingly high number wouldn't know the difference between two leg and inside leg.

Last of all, as in the New Football Culture, the anorak lives on. This is an essential point to grasp. All real cricket fans are anoraks at heart. With so many statistics involved in even a superficial understanding of the game, it would be unnatural if they weren't. They can quote batting averages and highest wicket partnerships with the best of them. The new cricket anoraks, however, have a life beyond the pages of *Playfair Cricket Annual*. That life probably includes a professional job, Oasis and Blur CDs, going to clubs, a tendency to support New Labour, regular reading of men's style magazines, and regular viewing of 'Fantasy Football League', 'The Fast Show' and 'Father Ted'. Having said this though, what they do beyond the jurisdiction of the ICC is not of great importance. It is cricket that counts, not the contents of your CD tower.

A lot of people will now be thinking: 'You arrogant bastards. Do you really think you're the first generation of cricket fans to have thought the establishment needed toppling and you are the people to do it. After all, my dad's sixty-seven and he thinks that Ray Illingworth's a tosser.'

And yes, it is hard to imagine any point in cricket's history when people weren't questioning the way things were being run. Do you suppose, for instance, that when England were being bounced around by Lillee and Thomson in the mid seventies, that people of the calibre of Peter Roebuck and Vic Marks were sitting in their Oxford Uni. charabanc saying: 'Doug Insole, what a marvellous chairman of the TCCB that man really is', or 'I think Mike Denness has done a pretty good job in really difficult circumstances'? I don't think so.

Peter Hardy – the founder and editor of the late-eighties groundbreaking fanzine *Sticky Wicket* says that many of his contributors were middle-aged professional people who relished the opportunity to say something challenging or controversial about the game. This is the key to the development of the mid-nineties cricket culture and the grand claims it makes for itself. It is not that nobody else has ever thought like we do. It is that nobody else has had the chance to give their opinions as we do. *Sticky Wicket's* contributors suddenly found a channel through which to express themselves. The development of the sociological phenomenon of New Laddism, Sky TV, cheap desktop publishing, and a host of other factors, means that we take those channels for granted. They are just there. In the mid 1990s, this is the established method for twenty- and thirty-somethings to express themselves. It is the norm. It is as simple as that.

In short, we are not saying that we are different from, or better than, previous generations. We just have more, much more, opportunity. So far, the New Cricket Culture is taking advantage of those opportunities. It has spawned two nationally distributed fanzines (*Sticky Wicket* and *Johnny Miller 96 Not Out*) and two fully-fledged magazines (*Third Man* and *Inside Edge*). It has a political hero in Mike Marqusee, author of establishment-baiting bestseller *Anyone But England*. (Just to rub salt in the wounds, Marqusee is not only a Marxist, but an American to boot.) Through the Barmy Army, it has made the way younger people support the game a media issue. The three leading lights of the Barmy Army also had the courage of their convictions to turn their ad-hoc nomadic cricket party of the 1994–5 Ashes tour into a leisurewear business the following summer. The Barmy Army (again) organised a second tour to South Africa in 1995–6. Their ultimate aim is to instigate an official England supporters club. Finally, following the 1995 'Henderson Affair' when an article in *Wisden Cricket Monthly* by Robert Henderson questioned whether black players should be picked for England, the New Cricket Culture was responsible for instigating the Hit Racism for Six Campaign aimed at eliminating this kind of prejudice from cricket. None of these things could have happened without the development of the New Cricket Culture, which in turn would not have arisen without the social changes in the 1990s that also gave rise to New Laddism.

So, what has been the cricket establishment's response to the

New Cricket Culture? Reactionary, in the extreme. *JM96** was banned by numerous counties. Counties refused to stock Barmy Army merchandise. The TCCB said this was a commercial decision to avoid competition with the counties' own branded products. *Third Man* got an excellent and supportive reception from parts of the cricket establishment and a downright hostile one from others. One senior official at a test match ground threatened us with police action while we were distributing promotional material outside the ground. He wasn't polite about it either. Having worked as a journalist on the police service trade magazine for nearly four years, I knew as much as he did that he was talking out of his arse.

The media's reaction to the Barmy Army and similar style supporters has been a little short of objective, even though in Australia, Dave Peacock and his fellow travellers were fêted wherever they went. They signed autographs for young Aussie cricket fans. They were even publicly thanked by the local cricket association at one of England's up-country games and given a mid-field ovation by the 4,000-strong crowd.

During the 1995 West Indies series and the following winter's tests in South Africa, you couldn't go half an hour without a radio commentary exchange between Jonathan Agnew and Trevor Bailey along the lines of: 'Tell me Trevor, how long do you think you could jump up and down chanting "Barmy Army" before you got bored?' 'Oh, I think about two seconds, Aggers.' Yeah, we get the picture, guys: Barmy Army, still mindless thugs. But mindless thugs who fielded a side in a charity game against a Development XI in Soweto and raised over a £1,000 for the development of township cricket through the sale of their T-shirts. Barmy Army members also note with cynicism how West Indian or Pakistani fans making a downright rumpus at matches are described as 'a colourful part of the local cricket culture', but the British are still 'soccer morons'.

In an uncanny echo of the Criminal Justice Act, which targeted raves and music characterised by 'repetitive beats' the Test and County Cricket Board began the 1995 season by issuing a classic sledgehammer and nut statement: '[The Barmy Army's] repetitive noise and chanting would be unacceptable in our grounds. We have regulations forbidding it and the waving of banners and flags, and we will be taking advice from the police.'

And how well test ground security enforced those regulations. On the Trent Bridge Saturday in 1995, the aforementioned twenty-strong male and female choir of Elvises delivered a note-perfect a cappella rendition of 'Return to Sender' during the afternoon drinks break, to the obvious delight of the rest of the crowd. The stewards' response was to confiscate the song sheets when the Elvises began handing them out.

Stewarding was even stricter at the Oval (the two London venues are much more sombre than those in the North and the Midlands). On the last day, as the series petered out to an undeservedly tame and dreary conclusion in a stadium filled to about one-third capacity, a group of supporters sitting right at the back of the low-level stands square of the wicket held up an inflatable Mr Blobby. It had been aloft for no more than thirty seconds before a steward was dispatched to remove it.

The authorities act like they don't want the fans there. It's a case of come and see the game, but only on our terms. They haven't yet had the gumption to ban the 'wrong' type of fan from the ground – they need the money too much. But Lord's is only a short step away from having the mechanism in place to do it. All test grounds apart from Lord's operate a first come, first served policy on test tickets. Lord's prefers a ballot. You send in your cheque and all the ticket applications go into a hat and the lucky ones get seats. It's not too difficult to imagine the names of the people sitting in row J, seats 17 – 25 of the Compton Stand who were seen waving Union flags, being looked up on the computer. The following year, those names would be automatically excluded from the ballot. Or better still, why not just eliminate anyone with an East London postcode?

Dave Peacock summed up the situation when he said: 'The cricket authorities are scared of us, but they don't know what they're scared of.' If they weren't scared of supporters like Peacock or magazines like *JM96**, then they wouldn't bother banning them. You only take action against things that are, or could become, real threats.

The one drawback in all this is that the New Cricket Culture is, to put it in the vernacular, in danger of disappearing up its own arsehole. So far, cricket's new generation has delivered less than it has promised. The opposite of gestalt, it has been a movement the whole of which has been very much less than the sum of its parts. To an extent those in the New Cricket Culture have been seduced by the success of New Laddism in general and by the successful model of laddish intellectualism in football.

Soccer also has *When Saturday Comes*, the ultimate fanzine success story. Spurred on by the success of *WSC* and the resurgence of an adult football culture, the major publishing houses soon jumped on to the bandwagon. Haymarket's *FourFourTwo*, launched in 1994, has men's magazines such as *Arena* as its model. This was followed a year later by *Goal* from IPC and Future Publishing's *Total Football*, both of which were New Laddism-inspired.

Cricket has nothing comparable in terms of sales success. *Sticky Wicket*, the first real attempt at an 'alternative' cricket magazine, launched at the tail-end of the 1980s could not survive when its founder and editor wanted to move on, even though it had the backing of one of the UK's leading contract publishing organisations, Viz publisher John Brown. *Third Man* – the short-lived magazine relaunched in 1995 and closed later that summer – aimed to emulate the intelligent analysis and presentation of *FourFourTwo* but didn't succeed.

The failures of *Third Man* and *Sticky Wicket*, when compared with the success and staying power of the establishment magazines the *Cricketer* and *Wisden Cricket Monthly* – universally acknowledged by adherents of the New Cricket Culture to be terminally boring – suggests one of two things. Either the products were wrong. Or the products were right for the minority readership they attracted, but that readership was an irredeemable minority, while the majority of cricket magazine readers were, and always will be, irredeemably boring.

In other words, the experience of the last few years is that the New Cricket Culture has not been big enough to sustain a mainstream magazine. But the New Cricket Culture is still in its developmental stages and this will not always be the case.

The publisher of *Johnny Miller 96 Not Out* decided to cease publication early in 1996 after six years of publication, but not because the magazine was failing. In fanzine terms it was ticking over nicely. They simply recognised that the New Cricket Culture was coming of age and that it needed a mainstream magazine which combined the irreverent approach of *JM96** with higher standards of journalism, photography and presentation.

There are fifteen-odd football magazines produced by the UK's four major publishing houses. There are countless cycling magazines and three dedicated to rugby union. Future Publishing has even put out a snowboarding mag, for crying out bloody loud. But none of them has ventured into cricket. It can only be a matter of time before IPC or Haymarket, say, bites the bullet and, with a vast promotional budget, wipes the floor with the *Cricketer* and *WCM*. There are many reasons why they haven't already done so. One of them is that they do not appreciate exactly what the New Cricket Culture represents.

One publishing executive I talked to believes that 'cricket is a middle-class game' and as a result cannot support the same approach taken by *Loaded*, *Goal* or *Total Football*. Another believes that there is less potential advertising revenue in cricket than there is in rugby. Yeah, a game in which you need to buy a pair of boots and a jock strap and you're ready to go will have more equipment advertising than cricket. A third believes that there is no scope for another magazine because the circulations of *WCM* and the *Cricketer* are falling.

As members of the New Cricket Culture, we know they are wrong. But remember that these are people whose professional *raison d'être* is to identify and research new magazines. If they cannot see the New Cricket Culture, it is either because it doesn't exist, which we know it does, or it is not yet visible enough.

This is the key. Football's New Culture is everywhere, Cricket's is not yet. Football lads are in *Loaded*, *Total Football* and *Goal*. They are creeping into magazines like *GQ* and *Arena*. They are on TV with 'Fantasy Football League' and 'Standing Room Only'. Yet the BBC doesn't even consider a cricket equivalent to 'Standing Room Only', a youth-presented TV fanzine. Instead we get the awesomely awful 'Gower's Cricket Monthly' offering us the wife of Leicestershire's Phil Robinson interviewing Hansie Cronje over a barbecue in her back garden. And even if the Beeb did go the visual fanzine route, who would they get to present it? Who are the cricket equivalents of Baddiel and Skinner?

Where is cricket's answer to *Fever Pitch*, the book that mines the deep wealth of common experience of soccer fans? The closest we have is Marcus Berkmann's *Rain Men*. It comes close to the reality – tuning in to Ceefax when 'TMS' is off the air, stopping to watch thirty seconds of silent footage in the TV shop-window – but at its heart, *Rain Men* lacks empathy with most of us. Marcus Berkmann and his team are a bunch of ex-Oxford no-talent park-cricket enthusiasts. I am a pretty good ex-Poly, borderline first team, south London club player. My experience is being sledged by the oppo's Aussie import or calculating the run rate you need to get a lousy draw in a rain-affected match, not poncing around in a stupid cap with Hugh Grant on the village green.

Oasis are obsessive about Manchester City; Blur follow Chelsea. But does Noel Gallagher support Lancashire? Does he even like cricket at all? Who knows? Sir Tim Rice, on the other hand, is a big fan of Denis Compton. Ryan Giggs is interviewed wearing a five-button suit or Nehru jacket. Mike Atherton wears, well, what? Nothing you'd see in *GQ's* fashion spread. I believe the term is 'sensible suit'.

Sean Bean starred in 1995's 'When Saturday Comes' as a Sheffield United soccer star. Cricket has 'Outside Edge'. Big fat hairy deal. Even when cricket can boast a part in alternative culture, such as the Acid Jazz record label's sponsorship of Surrey (Adam Hollioake and Neil Kendrick were seen driving around South London in Acid Jazz jeeps), you'd be hard pressed to find a general cricket follower who knew about it, much less understood its significance.

These examples all point to the fact that the New Cricket Culture, at the present time, has yet to command the influence it deserves. Or perhaps that should be, the positive influence. For there are plenty of times when the establishment and the press have been able to seize upon the worse aspects of cricket Laddism. Everyone knows about the disproportionate level of press vitriol generated by some pretty harmless chanting by the Barmy Army. The establishment has an open agenda in confronting this type of spectating. Yet there are times when it is handed ammunition on a plate.

Cricket's new culture embraces, sometimes reluctantly, the type of fan to be found on Headingley's Western Terrace, pissed by start of play, usually in fancy dress, and very, very vocal. The New Cricket Culture is right not to reject them, pointing out that fans such as these are part (although far from all) of the future of the game. Yet there are times to draw the line.

Booze talks and sometimes it talks independently of the brain. During the course of the rain-affected Leeds Test against the West Indies in 1995, over a hundred people were ejected from the ground. I saw one of them go. He needed five stewards to do it, one holding each limb and another his head. At one point in the raucous post-lunch session, a St John Ambulance woman had to walk to her assigned duty point. This took her on a course in front of the Western Terrace. This St John volunteer was overweight, a fact not lost on the intelligentsia in the stand, who decided to serenade her. 'You've had all the pies, you've had all the pies, you fat bastard, you fat bastard, you've had all the pies,' they sang.

The cricket establishment is outraged by behaviour such as this. They say it is not the way to behave at a cricket match. But that is an example of sporting snobbery that misses the point. It is not the way to behave full stop, irrespective of whether it's at a test match, Premier League game or Covent Garden opera. When the establishment throws up its hands in disgust and proclaims how disgraceful the new-style of cricket fan is, what better way could there be of drawing the establishment's thunder than for those very same new-style cricket fans to say 'we quite agree'. It is also a little ironic. After all, the New Cricket Culture had little difficulty in generating the Hit

Racism for Six Movement in the wake of 1995's Henderson affair. What is so different about hitting sexism for six? Or just downright unacceptably thuggish behaviour?

The New Cricket Culture is also partly defined by an us-against-the-establishment mind set and this has led to Mike Atherton receiving almost unquestioning support over his many misdemeanours during his tenure as England skipper. It was perceived that Atherton, because of his youth and hard-headed approach, would restore England's fortunes, and his frequent clashes with authority meant that (in line with the doctrine of my enemy's enemy is my friend) Atherton's hero status increased.

The New Cricket Culture has seen two high-profile failures. The Barmy Army merchandising business made a loss and was wound up at the end of 1995. And at the time of writing the organisers of Hit Racism for Six were gearing up for campaigning for the forthcoming season, but still had not received official recognition (whereas football's equivalent has the full backing of the FA). Counties and boards have refused to meet with them, they've received poor publicity, and many early supporters have lost their motivation now that the Henderson affair that provided the impetus for the campaign has blown over.

If these last couple of thousand words seems overly critical, downbeat and pessimistic, they are not meant to be. They are merely meant to put into context what is still a developing movement. There is plenty of work to be done, and the new breed of cricket fans have to recognise this fact and go about putting it right.

Revolutions do not happen in this country. Institutions here do not fall at the point of a bayonet. They fall as a result of several Swiss army knives gradually chipping away at their stone edifices. That is what is happening to the cricket establishment in the last decade of the second millennium. And that is where the real power of the New Cricket Culture lies. In the clash between Utopianism (the new culture) and Reactionism (the establishment) no one will achieve absolute victory. Hit Racism for Six could never have succeeded by telling the old dodderers in the MCC that they were racist beyond redemption. They would just have pulled down the shutters, whinged about lefty intellectuals invading our game and, well, that would have been that, barriers up on both sides. Hit Racism for Six will succeed, however, by constantly reiterating that racist behaviour is not acceptable, while pointing out examples of institutional racism. It has, perhaps, more of an educational role than a revolutionary power for change.

If the New Cricket Culture does do its job properly, the cricket establishment will soon have to accept that the way people support the game is changing irreversibly and that the new supporters have a voice and are using it. Utopians cannot control change, but neither can Reactionaries stand in its way. The days have long gone when cricket's authorities could fill up a ground with paying spectators who would do as they were told. It was people power that forced the TCCB to introduce wet-weather refunds. The protests that followed the abandonment of play in a 1992 test against Pakistan after just two balls in the day – refunds were available only if the entire day were washed out and 89 overs and four balls was not an entire day – were so vehement that even the TCCB could not sweep them under the carpet.

More importantly, the very state of the game itself dictates that the cricket authorities have to accept change or lose their power. The game needs money. To get money, you need paying spectators at the gate or paying viewers on TV. There is only one source of these new paying customers: the audience that watches Sky, follows football, is young and has no pretensions to egg and bacon ties and panama hats. In short, they are already New Lads and so perfect potential members of the New Cricket Culture. The cricket establishment is on the horns of a dilemma. They want more people to follow the game, but don't want the type of new cricket lover they are most likely to attract. They are happy to sell rights to international matches to Sky and reap the financial benefits, but far from happy with Sky's audience profile. Sorry TCCB, you can't have your cake and eat it too.

At some point in the near future, the establishment and the New Cricket Culture will meet in some yet-to-be-defined middle ground. Perhaps in the first or second decade of the next century, flag-waving, chanting, barracking, fancy dress adorned spectators will be seated in sections of test match grounds purposely given over to them. They will read a bestselling cricket magazine aimed at twenty to thirty-five year olds with a serious interest in all aspects of the game, not some anorak who needs his fix of Minor County scores for that month. They will watch an England team managed by a former international cricketer who has only recently retired from the game. They will accept that cricket shares the same glamour and appeal in popular culture as football did at the end of last century. The fans in 2005 or 2015 will take all this for granted and marvel how it could have ever have been different. I mean, fancy letting some bloke who'd been out of the game for twenty years run the national squad. Bloody ridiculous.

This will happen. There is no doubt about it. And the pioneers of this change will have been Dave Peacock and the Barmy Army, *Sticky Wicket*, Mike Marqusee, *Johnny Miller 96**, *Third Man*, *Inside Edge*, Alison and Charlie Mellor, you and me. This is the real power of the New Cricket Culture and this will be our real legacy.

3

FROM GAZZA TO DAZZA
Philip Cornwall

Wayne Larkins will always be one of my favourite footballers.

It was in the autumn of 1984 that Ned completed a unique double, becoming the only player to turn out for both Northamptonshire and Buckingham Town, thereby cementing a permanent place in my Hall of Fame. At last, the Robins had a player other people might have heard of, and for the first time I was able to watch a Northants player finish regularly on the winning side. He remains the only Northants player I've ever seen get a hat trick and, sadly, the only one I've ever seen win a championship (Nene Group United Counties League Premier Division, 1985–6).

Here was a major international sportsman – look, I'm a Northants fan – playing at a ground where supporters could indulge in that rare pleasure of kicking the ball back out of the net after someone scored (as we still can at one end). Not that he appeared to play the big star. As a batsman used to scoring mostly in boundaries, the concept of running had evidently passed him by. But his regular ambles into the penalty area showed willing and had the desired effect; better still, as time wore on, Wayne worked at his game and improved. Thirteen league goals in the first season – twenty-two behind John Frost – seem to have consisted mainly of spring-haired headers from set pieces, but in 1985–6 he was a yard quicker than the year before. Perhaps he'd abandoned his trademark cricketing practice of stubbing out his cigarette at the last possible moment before entering the field of play. Whatever, as England's 1985–6 tour of the Caribbean disintegrated amid splintered stumps and bone, Wayne top-scored with sixteen in a more defensive line-up. It was an impressive total in a season foreshortened by cricket and injury, and it helped us earn a promotion to which we've clung stubbornly ever since.

This was a golden age for Buckingham Town – two titles and an FA Cup tie with a league club in three seasons. The summers in between were part of a depressing era for Northamptonshire – one top-half Championship finish in nine seasons and the NatWest semi defeat by Middlesex in 1984 which was the closest we came to one-day success between 1981 and 1987. And though Buckingham have only ever been watched by handfuls, the same is true of Northants. Northants's seasons regularly came to an end in July or early August, while the Robins were as competitive in April as in September.

The Robins' home, Ford Meadow, was primitive then (and now), but it has a beautiful undeveloped view across the town. This was surely the envy of the County Ground, which appeared to be strategically placed so that the green of nearby Abingdon Park is completely obscured. The Wet Monday at Derby is still an experience I've been spared, but visitors would regularly remark on the ugliness of our ground in comparison, fairly or otherwise. They still do, of course, but the 1985 version was not a patch on the facilities on offer today.

Football was an integral part of the Northants experience at that time, with the ground disfigured by the Cobblers' bare terracing and floodlights and the club forced to start the home season late and finish early to accommodate the footballers. And so the two seasons flowed seamlessly, one into the other. And where was the passion, the noise, the sense of success and achievement? While Allan Lamb regularly made the step up from county squalor to England affluence, it seemed to me then that Wayne was involved in a more meaningful sporting contest when he took on Irthlingborough or Rushden than when even the star-studded Somerset side came to Wantage Road. There might have been more money at Northampton, but no one ever fell asleep watching Buckingham Town.

Even before Wayne Larkins, football and cricket had always had a lot in common. Both are games Britain gave to the world in the last century and which the world has stubbornly refused to give back to us ever since. More recently, at the top of both games at least, the money-changers have come into the temple and no one has been powerful enough to overturn their tables. Television's control over both sports has reached unthought-of proportions. The numbers and type of people who follow either game have been dramatically effected by both changes in the sports themselves and in the nature of late-twentieth-century society. The style and the nature of press coverage has also altered, partly reflecting, partly causing these other changes.

A decade before Wayne's arrival at Ford Meadow, it was fairly clear where cricket and football were going – nowhere fast. Declining attendances and national teams were the clearest indications A decade later, only someone willing to risk selling a Brian Lara spread bet would put money on the current competitive structure of either sport surviving to the year 2000. The home viewer is putting more cash into football than the crowd at the game, who in turn may be spending more on the commercial side than on match tickets. Sponsorship deals and commercial activities at test level have seen the Test and County Cricket Board subsidy to individual counties increase from around £100,000 to close to £1 million in little more than ten years. And footballers who can turn their arm over, or cricketers who can use their head, can no longer cross the divide for fear of the insurance companies.

Football and cricket have always been subject to evolution, but, taking a historical perspective, it seems to me that the changes in television brought about by and wrought upon the two sports constitute a revolution in itself that needs examining. Television now dictates when matches start and finish and what competitions are played. It even effects, in the case of sudden death extra time and the rain farces of the 1992 World Cup, the rules of the games and possibly thereby the results.

Perhaps surprisingly, the TV coverage of cricket had much more influence on football than the other way round. This was far from clear at the time – the time being 12 – 17 March 1977; the place, the Centenary Test between Australia and England at Melbourne. Gradual changes in cricket had come about partly through declining crowds, partly through changes in the media. But then came Kerry Packer and gradual changes were as passé as walking.

Imagine, for a moment, that it is the late 1970s and you are a television executive – or, if you wish to feel more human, imagine that you are a Martian orbiting the earth, wondering why there are so few communications satellites making the trip with you. Either way, you are planning an invasion: looking for the next Big Thing in broadcasting. A friend of yours has looked at the successful plot but limited appeal of 'I, Claudius' and has come up with the idea of the global glamour soap opera. But you are looking to save on the cost of scriptwriters by coming up with something with the unpredictability built in. Sport.

American sport makes huge amounts of money, but interests no one who is anyone outside the USA. The Olympics are the biggest thing anywhere, but the problem is that what makes them special is the fact that they take place every four years. The same applies to the (football) World Cup, but unlike the Olympics, the staple content is popular all the time, the zenith of the World Cup almost matched by equal peaks of interest in each country with cup finals and so forth. Regular club football attracts hundreds of thousands week in, week out for well over half the year, across the majority of the planet's land mass. All that stands in your way are a few amateur administrators and the scruples of those few club owners and players who can't be bought out. You could make a mint.

But Kerry Packer was an Australian, an inhabitant of one of the few countries where the word football brings to mind a ball that won't bounce straight. And this was a time when a clutch of Australians were international cricket stars with charisma rarely found among those so often dubbed 'sports personalities'. Lillee, Thomson, Marsh, Greg and Ian Chappell, Walters and others were larger than life, and the same could be said of half a dozen from some other test countries. The one-day international, brought into being by the Melbourne weather in 1970, at last offered a bite-size version of the game, and the first cricket World Cup in 1975 had provided, in its dramatic climax, an idea of what could be achieved. The apartheid boycott was depriving the international game of a few world-class players altogether, so finding a way to bring these outsiders into the game at the highest level would be offering something not available elsewhere. As the cricket authorities wouldn't negotiate with Packer, he decided to cut out the middle man – or, rather, to get England captain Tony Greig to personally recruit the players he needed for his very own sports soap opera.

It was Jim Laker who memorably dubbed the 1980 Centenary Test 'a unique occasion, really – a repeat of Melbourne in 1977.' But the Bastille was only stormed once, and it is that collision of true amateurism and professionalism at its most tawdry which establishes Melbourne as the landmark match.

I watched the highlights of that Melbourne match on 'Grandstand', between 'Football Focus' and setting out for the big match at Ford Meadow. Already under threat from one-dayers, cricket was being undermined from within. But on the pitch, Derek Randall was dragging the most unexpected of reactions from an Australian side not known for its manners. My naïve nine-year-old's idea of sportsmanship seemed to be defined by Rodney Marsh recalling Rags after the umpire gave him out off one that didn't carry. Captain Greig, however, was setting in train events which would make such gestures as much an historical curiosity as Randall himself. Events as influential on football as on cricket.

The lesson Kerry Packer preached – Money talks – was not a new one. The problem with cash, of course, is that the more anyone gets, the more they appear to want. But sport had, to some extent, always managed to protect itself from making too much money. In the long run, Packer failed to heed his own lesson, or at least his lack of media interests outside Australia, and the restrictions, pre-satellite, on the number of available channels prevented him from fully exploiting the gap he had created. But he won. While World Series cricket as an outlaw organisation did not live that long, that's because the authorities surrendered to Packer and the players, not the other way round. One day, someone used that victory as an acknowledged stick with which to beat the TCCB, the Football Association and anyone else who got in his way. Today's situation, with Rupert Murdoch controlling several 'whole new ball games' based on the success of his deal for English football, is a result of battles won by, or on behalf of, Kerry Packer. And what happened next in terms of player freedom within both sports also owes a certain debt to the Packer era.

This new compromise – that the sporting authorities would surrender a degree of control over the game in exchange for money, in order to keep the game under one umbrella – was not the only one set by the Packer circus. The gentlemen of the MCC woke up, wandered, blinking in the sunlight, from the Long Room to the Law Courts, and assumed that their confrères on the bench would back up their historic right to control the game. Instead, the set-back they received revived the principle that sportsmen and women had legal rights they did not surrender simply by virtue of being born talented. From now on, the players would be on a much more even footing.

These twin precedents – that television can go directly to those who actually do the entertaining if the authorities won't give them what they want and that the 'laws' of a sporting body are worthless when confronted by the legal authority – established a new set of rules in sport. This set of rules was ever more ruthlessly applied in football through the 1980s and 1990s, resulting in events which in turn have completed the circle by altering the terms under which cricket operates.

At first, attempts by clubs at the top of English football to cash in on their success by breaking away from existing structures foundered on the game's unpopularity with the advertising fraternity. Even when deals were struck, such as Canon's sponsorship of the Football League, they were liable to founder on companies' reluctance to be tarred with the brush of hooliganism. Nonetheless, the previously cosy relationship between the BBC and ITV was broken up and the sport made more money.

Then fate played a part. In early 1990, Sky Sports was very much a joke broadcaster, its schedules filled with glorified tiddlywinks. Incongruously, the satellite repeats station, UK Gold, frequently screens the episode of the spoof KYTV in which S(KY)'s early sports output is lampooned. Live coverage of England's overseas test matches was the one prestigious item on Sky Sports's line-up, and the rights were only available because the terrestrial broadcasters didn't have the airtime to show them. The prospect of watching England cave in to the West Indies yet again was hardly appealing, either. Highlights would be more than sufficient, and what would Sky show on days four and five, with the matches long since over? Dishes were as socially unacceptable in polite company as liking football. And then, from nowhere, came 'the miracle at Kingston'.

Devon Malcolm, Angus Fraser and Allan Lamb produced the performances that enabled England to win a test match against the West Indies for the first time in sixteen years, one Wayne Larkins eventually striking the winning run. Cricket became a product people were actually interested in watching and paying to watch, at least as far as getting a dish was concerned. A hard-core sports fan, I should have been in Sky's target audience. Until 1990, they missed me completely.

And then came Gazza. It is difficult to appreciate the scale of the sea change in the popularity of a game that had been through Heysel and hooliganism, Bradford and Hillsborough. Perhaps the best indication were the words of Bernard Ingham, symbol of a government whose antipathy to the game knew few bounds, on 'Question Time' the evening after England's February 1995 game in Dublin was abandoned due to organized, extreme right-wing violence. Where once blanket condemnation would have been demanded by politicians and audience alike, Ingham's carefully constructed answer was based on the reality that football's problems stemmed from a minority who should not be allowed to wreck the game's reputation. Before 28.5 million people watched England play West Germany in the 1990 World Cup semi-final, football had no reputation to ruin.

Sky now had a product which increasing numbers of people liked and another which was becoming more popular. When you woke up in the middle of the night to decipher 'Test Match Special' from New Zealand, if you listened carefully you could hear the theme from The Godfather coming from the telly in the corner. Television's mafia were coming, making you an offer you couldn't refuse. Sky's cricket coverage reached a new level with the exclusive deal for the 1992 World Cup (after months of ifs and buts, it was installed in the office just in time). Subscriptions as well as a dish and decoder were now needed to watch. Would enough people pay? England duly obliged once more by reaching the final for another heroic defeat, shifting dishes in numbers to which films released straight to video and repeats of 'The Waltons' could never aspire. Cricket proved that sport was the number one dish driver; now Sky moved to acquire football, the number one sport. And thence, via assorted 'whole new ball games', to a situation in which even free-market Tory MPs worry about the power Rupert Murdoch now has in negotiations with sporting bodies. And all because an Australian TV executive, relatively unknown outside his own country, wanted the rights to broadcast a sport that many thought would soon be relegated to obscurity.

Something else happened to cricket in 1977 that had a long-term impact on the way in which cricket is portrayed. Ian Botham's arrival in test cricket as a player was explosive enough. Within a few years, his brio and brilliance put him head and shoulders above any domestic cricket rivals for a generation either side. And, like George Best in the sixties, who demonstrated a similar level of superior skill in football, Botham became, in the eyes of the press, far more than a back-page hero. Botham was perhaps the first cricketer whose whole life became a press story. It's hard to imagine Bob Willis, or even Tony Greig, figuring as a serious sex symbol.

A tabloid editor can never have enough scandals. You can save them up for lean spells and the run-up to elections or push them out if your rivals come up with a real beauty to lure back readers. What Ian Botham did, unfortunately for him as a player at times (though it's always helped his media career), was to make cricket a subject from which the press would try to squeeze scandal. Football leant itself to the front pages for years when there was a real story; match-fixing scandals, pre-Best, were major news. Cricket, too, could capture the front pages – just ask Basil D'Oliveira. But with the gradual shift in news values towards an era in which a newscaster can be flanked by a man dressed as a bunny rabbit, the papers with the highest readerships increasingly look for stories involving drugs, gambling, sex, or better still all three: stories of no more than transient importance, but which would sell a few more dailies to people who should know better. With 'sexy' the all-purpose adjective for whether a story will sell papers, Ian Botham has paved the way for someone as uncharismatic off the field as Phil Tufnell to become a front-page lead; and a similar decline has been seen in the coverage of back-page issues.

After all, off-field antics – the kind which tabloid hacks have a knack for tracking down – have been seen as causing poor on-field performances, even as grounds for ending a career: Did Mike Gatting wind up losing his job as England captain because Ian Botham had attracted the flies? The increase in news journalists covering sport has made conventional sports reporting much more difficult: footballers and cricketers alike do not differentiate between the two kinds of hacks, leaving us with an air of perpetual mistrust of anything but the most fawning relationship.

The build them up, knock them down syndrome is as

prevalent in cricket as it is in pop music or politics: players burst on to the scene and are hailed as the best thing since sliced bread; the next moment, they are considered the worst thing since expanded polystyrene packaging for soggy sandwiches. The emergence of a star can be determined as much by sex appeal as by successful appeals. Angus Fraser, the most boring England bowler since Bob Willis, had an almost identical test record to Darren Gough at the point in his career that Dazza has now reached. But what will the tabloids' reaction be if (a) Gough ever becomes fit again and then (b) is passed over as frequently by the selectors?

The authorities will, likewise, use those players with news value to market the game – while reserving the right to punish them if they attract certain kinds of headlines. They appear to pay little attention to the fact that, given the nature of human frailties, it is more likely that the player who is heavily marketed for back-page reasons will wind up on the front cover.

The nature of cricket, taking up whole working days, means that few beyond the retired or gentlemen of independent means can even imagine attending a majority of home games, unlike a football fan, whose season ticket is used at every opportunity. Much of what we absorb about the summer game – and I don't mean the rugby Super League – has to be derived from the media. But sitting at home in front of the box, or reading about the game the next day, is not, for me, The Real Thing. There are no finer words in the English language than 'I Was There'.

Sadly, I wasn't there at Headingley in 1986, a defining moment when football's influence on the behaviour of cricket fans, for a while intermittent, became more marked. As did the reaction to it.

England lost the second consecutive test of a three-game series to India. Bill Athey top-scored for the home side with an apologetic 32 and the words of *Wisden* were harsh indeed: 'The respective wicket-keepers made an excellent impression....The same, regretfully, can not be said of those spectators who tried to recreate the 'human wave' effect by synchronised waving of the arms....Their mindless imitation of the football crowds at the World Cup in Mexico did not help the batsman's concentration and left Headingley's reputation as a ground for cricket lovers as much in tatters as the reputation of the England team.'

Similar condemnation came in the daily press at the time. Later the same year, I was there at the Oval for the final test with New Zealand. On a dull Saturday, the light was a constant threat, while England were batting in search of a series-drawing win. When the players headed towards the pavilion in the late afternoon, boos rang out – until it became apparent that this was in fact a drinks interval. More likely Bovril than barley water. The Wave sped round the ground in celebration of the fact that the players were not retiring – and as a much needed restorative for the circulation; the *Telegraph* divided and misread the two reactions, depicting the boos as a criticism of the players for taking a drinks break on a dull day, and the Wave as an indication of boredom.

The appearance of the Mexican Wave at cricket grounds is a distinctive milestone on the road to the constant rhythm of the Barmy Army for two reasons. It is a piece of crowd participation that does not depend on what is happening on the pitch – classic football fan behaviour – and it was condemned by the game's establishment and its supporters in spite of being completely innocuous, as long as it was not in the batsman's line of sight.

The excesses of spectators at and around football – drunkenness, abuse, fighting – had appeared at cricket grounds from time to time. The area in front of the Tavern Bar at Lord's was rebuilt so that you couldn't see the wicket from the queue, in reaction to trouble at one-day finals. The attempts by the cricket establishment to bracket what they thought of as 'anti-social behaviour' with the kind of outrages too often seen at football matches during the 1980s had occasional merit. But to condemn the type of celebration that wouldn't attract a second glance at Highbury or Anfield was perverse.

Perverse because the last ten years have seen a clear attempt by the cricket authorities at local, national and international level to try and breed a fan culture more akin to that of football. Just as the *Telegraph*, the last paper with a reporter at every ground, realised it had to modernise as its traditional readership was dying out, so cricket realised that at a time when its audience was in decline, it needed to borrow from sports which were attracting the young in numbers. Not that football has worried about borrowing in the opposite direction.

Cricket in its purest form – or at least that form favoured by the 'purist' – is not very helpful to the employed. Football is conducted outside the normal working hours of surely 90 per cent of the population: the traditional 3pm kick-off on a Saturday derived from an estimation of how long the working man would need to get home and eat after doing his Saturday half shift before heading for the game. Whether consciously or not, the introduction of the one-day game tried to offer cricket at similarly convenient times, with the guarantee of a result from, at most, one day off work for the midweek games, or as a Sunday afternoon out. Cricket was the first major sport in this country to make full use of Sunday, and in the 1970s and 1980s it was consequently broadcast in a programme more likely to be called 'Sunday Cricket' than 'Sunday Grandstand'. In time, of course, every other sport, including football, followed suit, to the extent that Peter West was driven off BBC 2, and a new way of enticing people to the game was needed. Introducing the

Refuge Cup didn't work. Sticking the games on Sky, guaranteeing that they would be shown but would be seen by no one, didn't work to the extent that the TCCB were forced to sponsor their own competition in 1992. So, coloured clothing and replica shirts, staples of football culture, became the order of the day at county level.

Internationally, of course, that was already happening. The England shirt from the 1992 cricket World Cup sold in thousands, and soon was as regular a sight at England football games as its Umbro counterpart had been at test matches. Tribalism, based on wearing the colours of your side, was the most visible sign of the attempts to borrow from football's new merchandising boom. And nowhere was it more visible than on tour. The Barmy Army was here, for good or ill, and was a creation of the marketing of the game, just as Ian Botham was used and condemned by the same people. *Loaded*, a magazine explicitly 'for men who should know better', finds valuable copy in both the players and the new supporters.

Following England abroad was once the preserve of the MCC member and his county equivalents. Can anyone remember hearing the cheers of England supporters at an away test before 1990? And yet those who pay so much to travel so far and enthusiastically support a team that performs abysmally with such alarming regularity remain pariahs to many of those who are used to having overseas tours to themselves and getting paid to go. Singing for your team is frowned upon, even when England are playing in countries where the local support is famously exuberant. The Barmy Army lets people know that they care about winning and losing, which somehow goes against the definitions of Englishness carried around by those who commentate on and write about the game, yet who are simultaneously more than happy for the locals to keep up their own constant rhythm. The new breed of supporters, bringing the enthusiasm of a football crowd to a cricket match, make the England team feel wanted, even in abject defeat; as long as the Barmy Army is there, the players will never walk alone. At times when they seem abandoned even by the selectors, no wonder they seem happy to accept the congratulations and commiserations of those fans who are never on holiday in Majorca when England have a game.

The timing of the Barmy Army's rise to prominence seems to me to be no coincidence. The outbreak of banners in the crowd, guaranteed to be seen at some point during the lengthy pauses in the day's play, shows the opportunity presented by Sky to say 'Hello Mum' from the other side of the world. The louder your support for the side, the more likely you are to be noticed by the camera with the wandering lens.

But this sort of committed, travelling support does have its dangers as well as its benefits for cricket. Anyone who has followed the England football team at Wembley and, especially, abroad knows that there can be a disturbing edge to it all. Circumstances – principally the fact that the national side was, in the wake of the Heysel disaster, the only English team allowed to compete abroad – created a situation in which many of the travelling supporters were well over the boundary between nationalism and xenophobia, miles away from any patriotic 'love of country'. Having watched alcohol-fuelled bigots demand that Norwegians understand English and refuse to accept local currency because it didn't have the queen's head on it, having listened to chants of 'There ain't no black in the Union Jack', and heard the Poles, of all people, asked 'Where were you in World War II?', I know that there can be a frightening level of racism, arrogance and ignorance, leading all too frequently to violence, among a minority of national team supporters. The travelling support, obviously enough, has a higher proportion of the over-dedicated. Whether at home or abroad, spending an expensive day's test play sitting next to a bunch of drunks, with obscene chants thrown in, can be incredibly off-putting.

And these are the images of overseas support on which the authorities appear to focus. What cricket fails to comprehend, possibly at its peril, are the side effects of blanket condemnation of those elements of football culture from chants to Mexican Waves, which have come into the game. By attacking harmless habits, they may repel the very people they have tried to attract; by creating the impression that cricket is attracting an anti-social minority, they will actually encourage more of them to turn up. The condemnations imply that those who have been repelled in the past by cricket's stuffed-shirt image need to learn to behave. Anyone who has shared a stand with drunken yuppies; or had beer poured on them from an executive box; or heard people comment that 'whatever you think about Syd Lawrence, he tries hard – for a spade,' knows that cricket's traditional sources of support can produce people at least as obnoxious as the most boorish of the new breed.

Cricket cannot risk alienating its traditional audience; at the same time, it needs the money of the new fan. Surely the fervent supporter, at county and country level, is to be welcomed, provided that he or she stays within the bounds of the law? Unfortunately, progress will always hit the buffers who represent the traditional county member and who are not a tolerant bunch.

Having carefully divided my own supporting habits in two – frenetic in the winter, comatose in the summer – I was frequently irked by the big match atmosphere at Northampton on those rare occasions when it was hard to find somewhere to sit. For instance, a NatWest quarter-final tie with Warwickshire in 1989 saw people wearing Birmingham City shirts stand on the football terrace, in spite of the fact that it barely faced the cricket pitch. Some appeared to be unaware of what round it was, how many overs were involved, or the identity of more than a handful of players. But they had made a contribution to the coffers of the game, and if they enjoyed what they saw and came back, then that understanding would come. (After all, I'd watched the highlights of the Centenary Test under the illusion that if a batsman had the words "not out" appear beneath him on the screen, then he'd be back in the pavilion next ball.) And if they made more noise than those from the posher parts of Edgbaston, so what? Efforts at controlling the behaviour of people at sporting events should be targeted at those practices that are genuinely anti-social, not by the standards of the MCC or of 'polite' society, but of the real world. Anything else risks not just accusations of hypocrisy, but also calls into question the whole attempt to repopularise the game.

What of the future relationship between the two sports? Where will they be by 2000?

Sadly, there will be no more Wayne Larkinses, crossing the divide between the two for a winter bonus, or footballers keeping fit during the summer months. Wayne missed the first month of the 1986 season thanks to his football injury; he was hardly match fit when another injury cost him a test recall. Andy Goram, the Rangers and Scotland goalkeeper, turned out for his country in the B & H. But a stop was put to that before he went the way of Wayne. The more money at stake in the two games, the less someone can be an amateur, playing one game for a living and the other out of love.

When the vernacular, marketing, style and presentation of the two games are indistinguishable, they will both appeal to the same part of the senses. And therein lies a problem for cricket: Why opt for something that is artificially being forced to resemble football, when you can have the real thing? In the mean time, vive la différence.

Another problem with money, in both sports, is that where cash leads, lawyers will follow. How long before a demonstrably wrong decision, by the administrators of either sport, will wind up in court – and how long will it take for a precedent to be followed up? The Jean-Marc Bosman judgement, brought under the Treaty of Rome's employment statutes before the European Court of Justice, has thrown football transfers into confusion, in spite of the fact that it was widely anticipated by everyone except the people who run the game. How long before a similar case under the competition regulations is brought against the TCCB? The inclusion of Dutch and Irish national teams in the NatWest Trophy could have unforeseen complications. What if John Emburey, rather than coaching England A for the winter, coached Holland to the World Cup before returning to England? Past experience, with Packer and with the European loophole that saw Kevin Curran and Ole Mortensen circumvent the overseas player rules, suggests that the cricket authorities will cope no better than UEFA and the FA are with the Belgian.

There will also be Rupert Murdoch, or his descendants, increasingly calling the shots, unless the sport as a whole calls foul. In spite of Packer, perhaps the relative unpopularity of cricket and its reliance on national teams will enable it to resist the worst excesses of the football clubs, whose individualistic greed knows no bounds. But what of the changing relations between clubs and country? In football, the former are in the ascendant; in cricket, they would not survive without the latter. Will real power in both sports continue to be hijacked by those who are involved with the most profitable part of the game? Quite probably.

But much of this speculation is, at best, idle. One thing is certain: neither sport will ever be the same again. The changes that the two have undergone, separately or hand reluctantly in hand, have been irreversible. Television will dictate more and more, at the expense of tradition; the one-day cricket game will never reject the gimmicks that are introduced; nor will football return to being a game played when Saturday comes. Stories with less and less sporting relevance will be accorded more and more significance; and there will be no more Neds, just Athers and Dazzas, Lambies instead of Leggas. The Judge will be retired; Smudger will be the best we can hope for.

And that, perhaps, is what I will miss most. Nicknames that made no sense, or which at least required an imagination or explanation. Jaffas will only come out of Israel. Show me a promising player's name today, and I'll tell you what he'll become known as, should he ever take a couple of wickets on television.

That's the problem with a Rags to riches story.

4

STUFF THE SANDWICHES
Michele Savidge

'Are you something to do with the catering?' asked Lt. Col. (ret'd) John Stephenson, former secretary of the MCC. He had sat himself next to me at a lunch held by the *Evening Standard* for the 1991 West Indian touring party and was trying, uncomfortably, to make polite conversation.

Rearranging my not inconsiderable nose into as haughty a sneer as I could manage and giving my sweetest girlie smile, I replied: 'Actually, I'm with the *Evening Standard*. I'm on the sports desk.'

I emphasised the words 'sports desk' to give him a clue, but it was obvious that he now thought I must be something to do with the clerical side.

'Do you know John Thicknesse (the *Standard's* long-serving cricket correspondent) then?' he asked.

I resisted the urge to tip some of the catering on to his lap. 'Of course. As I'm a sports sub-editor, and my main interest is cricket, I sometimes rewrite his copy.'

'Do you really?' the astonished Lt. Col. queried, looking for all the world as though I had just told him that Ian Botham was a homosexual.

By all accounts, Lt. Col. (ret'd) John Stephenson is a real poppet, and compared to many other remarks I've faced over the years – since my first job as editorial assistant on the

Cricketer in 1982 –this exchange was really quite inoffensive.

However, it does beg the question: Why are women, catering and cricket so inextricably linked? Historically, it seems to have been assumed that women were unable to think of anything they would rather do than rustle up a few sandwiches and cakes for the weekend. There is even a book about cricket teas. Indeed, I have a very dear, liberated friend who can barely wait for the start of a new season as it provides her with the perfect opportunity to try out a new quiche recipe. Equally, it is automatically assumed by her husband and his friends that she and her fellow wives relish their roles as summer bakers. And yet these are women who in everyday life are intelligent business people!

I know club cricketers who even judge the success of their visits to other clubs not just by the results, but by the quality of the food. Next season, given the choice between a soggy sausage roll bought from Safeway or a homemade Dundee cake, you know which fixture is going to get the thumbs up. It seems that all cricketers, at whatever level, simply love a good tea – and more. Just look, if we must, at Mike Gatting: the perfect example of a player devoted to his caterers. Indeed, the legendary Nancy Doyle's influence on the dining room during thirty years at Lord's is spoken of with the utmost reverence.

But it is nothing less than distinctly peculiar that, in the late twentieth century, there are still legions of unreconstructed men who believe that after the bedroom (or even before) a woman's place is in the kitchen. It is even more odd, if not downright sad, that there are still intelligent women who go along with this head-in-the-oven attitude.

Of course, we all know that a game of cricket, unlike other sports, can occupy a fair stretch of time, hence the need for sustenance, and therefore a man could hardly be expected to knock up a quick spag Bol in between overs. But you would have thought that even an unreconstructed one could slap a couple of sandwiches together before he begins his weekend cricket pilgrimage. Or how about a quick trip to the thinking woman's life-saver: M&S? It is time to stuff the sandwiches.

Much too revolutionary, I know, because more than any other sport, including rugby, cricket is sorely over populated by more than its fair share of old farts and sexists. Cricket is for men; cooking is for women.

Speaking as a cricket journalist who has written about the game for nearly fifteen years, I can report that the higher reaches of cricket administration are littered with men sharing a tomato-stained old school tie, men who have only a blurred concept of the world outside their bifocals. And as one of these old buffers reaches his terminus, there is little imagination shown in appointing his replacement.

'I know the ideal chap,' says the committee chairman. 'Commander Bloggins, played for Cranberry in 1949.' Bloggins gets the job, the men of '49 stick together and English cricket maintains its blinkered mediocrity.

Until the last of the Bloggins clones has departed, the higher positions in cricket administration and management will be closed to younger men, let alone women. This is despite the fact that more women than ever before are taking an interest in the game, certainly at international level, and that more women are forging ahead of men in a wide range of professions.

But can you imagine a woman ever holding a senior management position in cricket? Could the equivalent of Karren Brady, the managing director of Birmingham City, ever appear in the 'sacred game'? Well, not if the Lord's hierarchy or half the cricket media have anything to do with it.

Take a look at sports journalism. Football boasts female reporters aplenty, while there are already female commentators on the radio, thanks to Radio Five Live. Sky TV even employs female presenters for soccer programmes.

Cricket doesn't yet enjoy such equality, although Radio Five Live has featured female cricket commentators, notably Joanne Watson, who has been ploughing a lonely furrow in cricket broadcasting at the BBC for years. Radio Five Live has been innovative in employing female sports presenters across the board and there is no reason to suppose that more women won't be employed in cricket radio broadcasting in the future. 'Test Match Special', however, may take a little longer!

Newspapers and television are another matter altogether. There is no sign of either a female cricket correspondent in the national press or, as in the West Indies, a female TV commentator. In fact, England even lags behind as unlikely a contender for equality as Pakistan, which boasts at least one national newspaper with a female cricket correspondent.

Although the situation in the UK has improved immeasurably, there are still some pretty unappetising barriers standing in the way of any woman determined to make her career in the cricket media.

In the dark ages of 1982, my first offer of a job was as a 'handmaiden' to a BBC journalist on that winter's tour to Australia. Even in my naiveté, I imagined the job would entail rather more than sharpening his pencil or polishing his calculator and declined his kind offer. And perhaps I shouldn't forget to mention, more recently, the former England spinner, in whose Rolls-Royce I was a passenger on the way to a business engagement, telling me 'You do know that I'm going to take you to bed.'

Actually, I'd had no idea, which shows how foolish I was. (Needless to say I ensured that he didn't!)

Then there was the even older former England player who asked me to go on holiday with him; and I musn't forget the rather well-known batsman who couldn't keep his clammy hands to himself or resist the urge to make some of the lewdest suggestions I've heard – all in a public place.

These examples are given simply to show how some cricketers seem unable to deal with the obviously burdensome amounts of testosterone which they might argue have enabled them to be so successful in their sport. Sadly, it had never occurred to them that a woman (they would say a girl) might be trying to make a serious career as a cricket journalist.

The press box, these days, is a lot more welcoming, thanks to the influx of liberal-minded youth. It is not too far-fetched to imagine that a female cricket correspondent, should a male sports editor ever be brave enough to take one on, could soon sit happily in the press box. Once there, however, she could come up against another problem: the increasing number of ex-players turned reporters, some of whom, as we have seen, regard a woman's rightful place as some distance from a cricket ground.

Of course, there are some former and current players who are not that kindly disposed to any journalists, regardless of gender, who haven't played the game. During an interview with Graham Gooch in the late 1980s, the former England captain said that someone who hadn't played the game didn't have the knowledge to write intelligently about it. (I wonder if, by the same rule, men can't be obstetricians then?)

This sort of attitude is problematic, particularly for women. The majority of male cricket journalists are assumed to have played the game at some level, but female reporters (whose mere presence is often a nasty shock in the matey atmosphere of a press conference) are never given the benefit of the doubt.

Personally, I prefer to go along with the leading article from a 1921 edition of the *Times* which proclaimed: 'We sincerely hope...that in future no one will be chosen to represent England except on the understanding that when he becomes a test match player he lays aside his pen.'

So the road to the top for women aspiring to enter cricket journalism is still a long one, despite the fact that fewer barriers exist today than perhaps at any time in the past. Just as women cricketers have not been taken seriously, neither have women cricket writers or commentators. In fact, the usual assumption has been that you're only there to look at the chaps.

Now, being a heterosexual woman (albeit a happily married one, with one child and another on the way) I confess that I can see absolutely nothing wrong with watching an attractive man playing cricket, the more attractive the better actually. But, let's face it, attractive men playing cricket are a bit thin on the ground, so that can hardly be the reason why so many women genuinely love the game. And certainly there appear to be more women at international matches now who are just as knowledgeable, some of them more so, as the men and aren't interested in how a cricketer looks, any more than the average male spectator would be. Many also go alone or with friends, male or female, rather than being dragged along by a husband or boyfriend. Indeed, increasingly, it is the other way around, with the wife or girlfriend being the keener follower of the game.

Very few of these female spectators are interested in women's cricket, with most finding the men's game more thrilling and absorbing than the women's version Many female cricketers too have found their inspiration in the men's game. Grace Williams, for example, the Jamaica and West Indies fast bowler of the 1970s, once spoke of being 'hypnotised' as a young girl by pace bowlers Wes Hall and Charlie Griffith. The latter was her hero and she endeavoured to emulate him in her game. In the book *Liberation Cricket*, Williams is highlighted as an example of the female players who 'learnt their cricket within the social context of the male game, and as a result identification with its heroes seemed inevitable.'

There are still many more women interested in watching cricket than in playing it. But that is true of the male population too. However, if a woman is to be successful at cricket she has got to show much more commitment than her male counterpart.

A girl might take up the sport as Kwik Cricket at primary school. But while local clubs are alerted to the presence of any talented boy, where does the girl go? The number of secondary schools offering cricket to girls is very small, so teenage girls who want to play the game really have to struggle to find any opportunities. Yet to think that in the eighteenth century women's cricket matches often entertained crowds of more than two thousand.

In England today, the number of clubs affiliated to the Women's Cricket Association is just over sixty with more sides playing in evening leagues. The WCA was formed in 1926, after which the number of clubs rose from 10 in 1927 to 80 by 1934 and 123 by 1938. At its peak in 1953 – the post-war boom evident here just as in other sports – the WCA boasted 208 clubs in England, Scotland, Wales and Northern Ireland, as well as 94 school and junior sides. The number of clubs then gradually diminished until a mini-revival occurred after England's victory over New Zealand in the World Cup in 1993, ending Australian domination of the one-day game.

For women who love the sport and excel at it, the game can become an expensive hobby. International players have to find money for flights, clothing and often equipment due to the lack of commercial sponsorship.

Elsewhere in the world the situation is little better, although in New Zealand women's cricket has successfully and profitably merged with the male system. There, girls and boys learn and play the game together and provincial associations provide organisation, facilities and coaching for both sexes.

Of course, there are many more women, not affiliated to any association, who more than play their part by participating in back yard cricket with brothers and sons. And don't underestimate their contribution. As just one example of many, Vic Richardson's daughter, Mrs Chappell, coached her three sons, Ian, Greg and Trevor in their garden.

And as Rachael Heyhoe-Flint was always keen to point out, it was a woman, Christina Willes, who invented overarm bowling after having difficulty bowling underarm to her brother because her voluminous skirt got in the way. Her brother devoted the rest of his playing days to getting the overarm action officially recognised. But at Lord's in 1822, playing for Kent against MCC, he was no-balled, threw down the ball in disgust, jumped on his horse and rode off never to play again.

His sister might be equally disgusted to discover that nearly 180 years later she would still not be allowed in the pavilion at this 'hallowed' ground. How can that be?

In 1990, the late Brian Johnston (hardly the most radical of cricket figures) proposed at the MCC AGM 'that women should be allowed to apply for membership of the MCC' and sponsored former England captain Heyhoe-Flint's application. The motion was roundly defeated and the possibility of 'egg-and-bacon' neck scarves being seen in front of the pavilion still looks bleak.

The pavilion at Lord's remains one of the few places in the world where women are not welcome as spectators. Another, the Kingston Cricket Club at Sabina Park in Jamaica, doesn't allow women to use many pavilion facilities, with the members' bar closed even to female West Indies players.

I have been watching cricket for about thirty years – and many women I know have been watching it for far longer – and neither I nor any of my fellow spectators regard my presence at a game as odd. In fact, the presence of women at international matches now raises no comment in the stands whatsoever.

Of course, there will always be the laddish, sexist comments from a small section of the crowd if a woman walks in front of the crowd during play. A man told me this was simple evidence of heterosexual male bonding in public. Well that's one way of putting it, I suppose. But there is still more evidence of the New Cricket Culture in the stands than in the media or the cricket administration.

Women in Ireland even have their own version of the Barmy Army: in fact, the 'Six Pack' have been around longer than the Barmy Army. Six Irish women dress up in costumes and follow the Irish women's team, laden with Guinness as they go.

Even the most loathsome City yahoo in the crowd won't question a woman's right to be in the stands. Contrast that with the stares or comments that are still being received in many pavilions. For women, it is far better to go along with this positive crowd culture than the negative pavilion culture. (That is one reason why I nearly always choose, and pay, to sit in the stands rather than in the press box).

But why are more women watching cricket? It is symptomatic of the society at large, in which more women work in a man's world and, for the first time in history, enjoy having their own money and making their own choices about how to spend it. As more women take up careers that have traditionally been thought of as exclusively male, so women choose to spend their leisure time just as men did in the past – watching sport. It is no coincidence that football is benefiting from a great increase in the number of female spectators, nor that you are just as likely to find business women on the golf courses as their male counterparts. One fifth of the subscribers to the long-running national cricket fanzine *Johnny Miller 96** were women.

Sport is finding a whole new audience, but some games have

been quicker to seize the opportunities than others. Football has been one of the first, running an advertising campaign in women's magazines to coincide with the 1996 European Championships. Has cricket tried anything similar? Well, what do you think?

What is cricket missing by not actively enticing women to watch the sport? For a start, half of the population is not being encouraged to go through the turnstiles: think of all the money that is being lost! Second, professionals such as physiotherapists and marketers – both areas in which many leading practitioners are women – are not being encouraged to bring their talents to the game.

But it isn't just money and skills that are being lost. No sport can flourish without representing the culture as it exists. Sport was a male thing but, in the 1990s, has ceased to be so. Cricket, with its administrators stuck in the 1950s, is failing to represent society and therefore has no alternative but to flounder in its present morass of despair and indifference.

In the past, almost the only chance a girl had of becoming interested in cricket was through her father, brother or, more rarely, her mother. And virtually the only chance she had of becoming involved in the game was by marrying a player. And just look at what that did for Frances Edmonds (and Phil).

But as more women become part of the New Cricket Culture, more will aspire to become involved at all levels of the sport. And if a football club can have a female managing director, if a rugby team can have a female physiotherapist, then what is there to stop cricket moving down the same advanced road? The Fred Flintstones of cricket cannot go on forever.

5

'A BIT LIKE SEX': LIFE ON THE COUNTY CIRCUIT
Martin Speight

'A bit like sex – it's fun for amateurs, but prostitutes don't do much laughing', *writer Hunter S Thompson describes his profession.*

From the age of eleven, my dream was to play first-class cricket for Sussex. I fulfilled this ambition seven years later in August 1986 in a match against Somerset at Taunton. I still have the press cuttings.

Somerset batted until lunch on the second day, and during their innings I took three catches behind the stumps. One of my victims was Joel Garner, out first ball off the bowling of Tony Pigott. But my most vivid impressions of that game remain the atmosphere in the ground when Viv Richards walked out to bat – the aura that surrounded the great man – and my anxiety at the prospect of facing Joel Garner, who, I naively imagined, would bowl even quicker to me because I had caught him the day before. I admit to being pretty relieved when it began to rain just after lunch, and didn't stop until tea the next day, by which time the ground was flooded and the match had been abandoned.

What more could an eighteen year old, fresh out of school and cricket-mad, ask for? Being paid to watch it rain and having the chance to meet Viv Richards, the greatest batsman of the modern era

For many young cricketers, joining the playing squad at a first-class county can be a revelation. After the end of my first Sussex second-eleven game, Paul Philipson (the second-eleven captain) gave me £25 to cover my match fee and meal allowance. I could not believe my luck. Not only had I been paid for doing something I believed to be a great privilege and would have done for nothing, but I had also been allowed a day off school to do it. As you can imagine, I was pretty pleased with myself; and this sense of achievement was further heightened upon my return to school, where news of my selection had spread like wildfire and I had achieved a kind of celebrity status.

'You are so lucky. I wish I played cricket for a living.'

If I was given a pound for every time I heard this during the ten years of my cricket career, I would be a rich man by now. Cricket is a great game and that is why millions of people give up their weekends to play club cricket. But few people realise that playing cricket for a living is not all fun and games. The reality is that professional cricket is exactly that, professional. It is a business to the management of each county club and a job to every county cricketer, and, as such, it can be very hard work.

Gone are the days of turning up at the ground half an hour before the start of the day's play, knocking back a few throw-downs and rolling over the bowling arm. Today, cricketers begin to prepare hours before play starts. On any Monday morning during the five months of summer about two hundred county cricketers arrive at a host of cricket grounds to play out the fourth and final day of their first-class fixture. By nine o'clock most will be struggling into their warm-up gear, aching from four solid days of cricket. Some will be lying on the physiotherapist's bench waiting to be treated. Those in the teams batting that day are thanking their lucky stars, while those fielding are invariably cursing their fate.

The atmosphere in the changing room inevitably depends on the previous four days of cricket – the first three days of the current first-class match and the previous day's forty-over Sunday league contest A win in the latter lifts everyone's spirits, but that is yesterday's news. The first-class match result is what really counts as both players and clubs are rated at the end of the season on their county Championship performance.

As in many careers in the 1990s, the demands on each player and team to succeed are significantly greater. Some argue that this is due to the increasing amount of money in modern cricket. Others claim that it is a result of more extensive media coverage or the current perception of winning as the only worthwhile goal in sport. Either way, everybody's expectations are that much greater. As Les Lenham (who played for Sussex between 1956 and 1970) admits, the pressures on current cricketers far exceed those of his day.

But probably you wouldn't notice any signs of pressure or tension on your Monday-morning visit to the dressing room. As the players drift in in groups of two or three, there is a fairly relaxed and jovial atmosphere. Usually a radio will be turned on, someone will be running a bath and the dressing-room attendant will have made a pot of tea. One of the players will be 'playing mum', pouring everyone a cup, and although most don't expect to be served, the opening bowler who is soaking his aching muscles in a hot bath will clamour for a cup for fear of being left out. Players chatter and joke about the bars and restaurants they've been to: which Italian restaurant serves the best pasta; which bar downtown is most popular on which night; who saw who with whom, where and when, and so on. Someone will have brought in a newspaper or two, and while one will have found its way to the toilets as valuable reading material – usually the *Sun* – the other, invariably the *Daily Telegraph*, is like gold dust.

There is always a queue of players waiting to look at the sports pages, but eventually this orderly system disintegrates and the curious will badger the paper's current possessor for information: Who scored runs?, and Who took wickets?, are the inevitable questions once the position of each game is ascertained. The answers are greeted with weak attempts at humour such as 'He can't bowl a hoop downhill!' or 'It must be a flat pitch if he got runs, my mum's better than him!' Invariably, somewhere along the line someone will dispute these criticisms and become the butt of these jibes in turn – 'Just because you went to university with him doesn't mean he's any good'. Bad jokes fill the air and lighten everyone's moods. People love to knock other people down to make themselves feel better, and cricketers are just the same. In this respect, the early-morning changing-room atmosphere can resemble any other place of employment before the day's work begins.

This social atmosphere is soon replaced by a realisation that there is a job to be done, a game to be won. Players still tell stories and swap jibes, but a more urgent feeling pervades the dressing room. The players in form are openly confident even before taking the field, predicting further successes, while those who are struggling show signs of worry verging on fear – fear of further failure. Nick Faldo once said that 'every potential disaster is a great opportunity in disguise'. Try telling that to a top-order batsman who is sitting on a pair.

Players struggling for form seem to fall into two categories. There are those who chatter incessantly, rarely sit still and feel that they have to be seen doing something, whether it be throw-downs, batting in the nets or bowling at a stump, to justify their place in the side. At the other end of the scale are those who sit in a corner pondering over yesterday's failure and worrying about today's challenge. All cricketers try to steer a path between these two extremes, but even the best players end up in one of these situations at some time during their career. Possibly the hardest thing in cricket is to totally believe in your own ability when form has deserted you. Only the exceptional players have the inate self-confidence of an Ian Botham, and the rest have to convince themselves that today is their day: even before they walk on to the park players have already put themselves under pressure.

By half past nine the atmosphere in the changing room bears little resemblance to that of the previous half hour. It's time to go to work. Feelings range from 'Oh no, here we go again' to 'Come on lads, let's get stuck in'. From now on most players start to think about their role in the day's play and how they are going to overcome the barriers before them. As a batsman, I think about how the bowlers will try to get me out and how I will respond. Each player has his own method of motivating himself. Although outwardly players try not to show that they care, inwardly success is all that counts.

As the start of play draws nearer, fielders and bowlers pray for quick wickets, and batsmen will themselves to score runs. I dare not think how many times I have prayed not to get a duck, and even when I have proceeded to do well, I still wish that I had scored more runs. For some reason I never seem to be truly happy, however well I have done.

Several years ago, when I was still at university, I was given a run in the Sussex side as an opening batsman during the summer holidays. I had failed on several occasions and was inevitably dejected by my lack of runs, and my feelings of depression deepened when I scored 1 and 0 against Nottinghamshire in the first game of the Eastbourne Festival. I must have been close to being dropped from the team when, in the second game at Eastbourne, I scored 88 against

Leicestershire. When I returned home that night, my parents were very pleased for me, but I was in as bad a mood as the day before. I felt I had been unlucky to have been dismissed and was angry that I had failed to reach my first first-class hundred. Is it any wonder that county cricketers' wives, girlfriends and families have a pretty hard time of it during the summer?

The players' dining room will invariably be a hub of socialising directly before the start of play. Players from both sides will sit and chat. At least one person will be having a look at the *Daily Telegraph* cryptic crossword, and others will join in, contributing a few tentative answers. If we're playing Glamorgan, Colin Metson, Steve James and Adrian Dale will have written in half the answers already and will refuse to help anyone else until they cannot do any more. Only then are they prepared to swap a few answers! If the crossword is still not completed, the only hope is that Alan Jones is umpiring. He is a *Daily Telegraph* cryptic crossword buff and he has usually completed it by breakfast. If even he does not know all the answers, there is always the opportunity of discussing the clues while fielding next to him at square leg. It certainly helps the day go quicker, and once the problems of the crossword are solved there is always cricket trivia.

Throughout the counties there are players who do crosswords, from the *Times* cryptic to the *Sun* two-speed. The away-team players invariably bring a number of newspapers to the ground, and a consortium of players will work their way through each crossword during the day. The *Sun* two-speed crossword is a good easy one to start with, followed by the purportedly simple '10-minute' crosswords in the other tabloids, and then a few players might graduate to a cryptic crossword.

Why do professional cricketers, especially batsmen, spend a large proportion of the day racking their brains trying to fill in crosswords? Batsmen would argue that they are more intelligent than bowlers – after all, who in their right mind would want to sprint thirty yards to deliver a cricket ball six times an over, twenty-five overs a day? Malcolm Marshall, during his first-class career alone, ran in 74,644 times in 408 games: about 1,000 miles just running in to bowl. The real reason is that batsmen spend a lot of time sitting around waiting to bat. It is inevitable that they get nervous, and by concentrating on the clues of a crossword, thoughts of failure can be pushed to one side, the mind is relaxed and the nerves are calmed.

Of course, filling in the answers to a crossword is not everyone's idea of a soothing pastime. Some players like to play their Gameboys, always trying to better their personal bests, while others like to relax by putting on personal stereos and listening to music.

Each individual has his own routine. Bill Athey, for instance, immaculately dressed in his whites half an hour before the start of play, will read a paper and drink a cup of tea. Franklyn Stephenson, on the other hand, will play a few notes on his guitar, strum the odd song or two, and only start to put on his whites at five to eleven when the rest of the team is walking out onto the ground. Now you know why Frankie was always last onto the pitch.

As a rule, the changing room immediately before a session is fairly quiet as the captain offers a few words of encouragement. At the start of the season there is excitement fuelled by a desire to succeed and secure the benefits that accompany success. By late August the atmosphere on and off the pitch depends to a large extent on the position of the team in the Championship. Teams with a chance of winning the Championship try to create an atmosphere and spirit that helps them achieve, while the others tend to go through the motions. The only thing that keeps these also-rans going is personal pride in their own performances. Although it is a sad indictment of the county game, it is hardly surprising. The physical and mental pressures on cricketers playing six or seven days a week, every week will have taken their toll by late August. Indeed, many players will be praying for rain so that they can have a day off.

Nowadays, however, rain is not a guarantee of being able to put your feet up. I would happily bet that the majority of county cricketers curse the person who invented the motorised sponge mop, which is used at most county grounds. Once it has stopped raining these machines can remove surplus water very quickly and play will start shortly thereafter. No longer do players and spectators alike have to wait hours for the natural process of drying by sun and wind. As a result, even if it has rained non-stop for hours on end, county cricketers have to remain at the ground for the majority of the day. During this time, players will watch sports and Australian soap operas on television; whoever is in charge of the remote control will regularly flick through Ceefax to find out who has scored runs or taken wickets elsewhere that day. Most county teams have a cards school and players gamble with their meal money and sometimes more, while a few players opt for backgammon.

Occasionally, if the match is abandoned for the day, players in opposing teams will try to arrange a 100-metre sprint race and bet on the outcome although all bets were off when you were playing Derbyshire and Michael Holding was in the team. In the past, Sussex players would try to pair up Colin Wells with the slowest runner in the opposition and his brother Alan with the quickest. Most teams knew that Alan was quick, but were quite prepared to contest a double header on the presumption that Colin was as slow as a cart horse. Unfortunately for them, Colin was far quicker than they realised; and it has often made me laugh that those that took on Colin were often prepared to give him a five-metre head start, only to see him stretch this lead further.

In 1987, Sussex played Kent at Maidstone and over a day had been washed out. I had taken to playing three-card brag, only to lose all my meal allowance within half an hour – I had backed a royal flush all the way only to lose to three queens. When a race between Alan Wells and Steve Marsh was arranged, I immediately agreed to back Alan to the tune of the money I had just lost on the cards. For some reason, only Colin and Alan himself agreed with my judgement, the rest thinking that Steve Marsh would be quicker. The Kent players raised £150 and we matched it – I was the main contributor. The course was measured out while the two runners warmed up. Fortunately, Alan was wearing half-spikes while Steve wore trainers; at the start, Steve slipped, giving Alan an unassailable lead. He duly cruised home first and I was back to my original financial state.

Betting, particularly on horses, plays a fairly large role in most changing rooms. Like most workmates, the Sussex players always have a sweepstake on the National and the Derby, but in addition a few cricketers have a flutter on the horses most days. Indeed, some players have the *Racing Post* or *Sporting Life* as their morning paper, and many a twelfth man has been sent to the bookies before the start of play to place bets on various tips accrued during the course of the season.

Just as players from different teams share tips on the horses, so they share other information as well. For some players it is the only opportunity of the season to meet up with friends playing for other counties and find out about their lives during the past year. Inevitably, the conversation comes around to cricket and the current state of the game, how it is affecting them, and how the administrators are tackling current issues.

It would not be difficult to guess that the majority of professional cricketers feel that they are underpaid and overworked.

This is a feeling that most people have at one time or another, but bearing in mind the short-term nature of a county cricketer's career and the big money earned by those in other professional sports, cricketers are undoubtedly poorly paid. The majority of cricketers earn little more than the £18,500 minimum wage set by the TCCB, and the only opportunity of securing a higher salary is to move to another county. However, unlike football, in which there is a relatively straightforward transfer system, this is not as simple as it sounds.

The majority of county cricketers are offered short-term (one- or two-year) contracts. When these have run their course, a county club has the option to renew a player's contract or release him. If the club releases a player, he is free to approach other clubs to attempt to secure another contract. If, however, the club offers the player another contract, he then becomes a List One player. This means that even if the player does not wish to take up the contract offered, he is often prevented from moving to another county. Counties are only permitted to offer places to two List One players from other teams every five years. As a result, if a county has its full quota of List One players, it is unable to employ anyone else in this category until the five-year period has elapsed.

These regulations were introduced to prevent the creation of a free-for-all transfer market. It was feared that a football-style situation would arise and that the wealthy county clubs would be able to buy the better players, thereby gaining an unfair advantage over the poorer clubs. However, many players feel that the regulations unfairly prevent them from maximising their earnings on the county-cricket labour market. It has been questioned whether these regulations contravene the Fair Trade Act; as yet no player has been prepared to risk taking them on, possibly for fear of future reprisals from the TCCB.

Over the past two years, the average county player's salary

has risen fairly substantially, although not as much as the players would have liked. County cricketers' salaries are paid over a six-month period – April to September – and rarely do these salaries pay enough to live on throughout a whole year.

Cricketers are in the minority of professional sportsmen who do not earn sufficient money in a season to cover the whole year. In any profession the top three hundred people earn very good salaries, and this should be the case with professional cricket. If players are expected to perform at the top level in any sport, practise is a key element. During the winter, most county cricketers spend time every week practising in the indoor nets and training in a gym to maintain and improve their fitness. This out-of-season work is even more vital for success in today's one-day-oriented game, and yet there is no financial reward for it. If the administrators of the game want the overall standards of county cricket to improve, thus boosting the standard of the players available to play for England, then players have to be paid all year round. This would give the players more opportunity to significantly improve their game. As yet, this is not the case, and as a result, the majority of professional cricketers have to find another source of income for the remaining six months. In today's economic climate, it is not particularly easy to find employment for the six months of winter, and bills and living costs still have to be paid.

For the top players, there is the possibility of being selected to go on one or two England tours, but for the majority of county cricketers, such an opportunity is rare. There is the option of going on the dole during the winter, and some are forced to do this. Another option is to try to secure a job abroad as a club professional.

Inevitably, the more successful players in county cricket secure the best deals with overseas clubs, mainly in South Africa, Australia and New Zealand. Neil Mallender, formerly of Somerset and now of Northamptonshire, has spent the last eleven years playing and coaching in New Zealand. The first ten of those years he played for Otago as their overseas player and was fortunate enough to receive a benefit there. This year he has wintered in Wellington, playing and coaching for the University Cricket Club. Roger Twose, formerly of Warwickshire, has played for three cricket associations in New Zealand. He has now emigrated there and plays not only for Wellington but also for the New Zealand test side, having served his seven-year qualifying period.

I have spent five summers playing and coaching for club sides in Wellington. I have been fortunate enough to secure reasonable contracts providing my return air fare from England, accommodation, a car and a weekly wage. On top of my coaching and playing commitments, I also work a thirty-hour week as a painter and decorator in order to supplement my income, but at no stage have I earned enough money to cover any bills at home. Any mortgage, pension and other bills have to be covered by my county-cricket salary. For younger, less-established cricketers, overseas coaching jobs are very poorly paid and they often have to meet their own air fares and living expenses.

But even if you can find a coaching job overseas that pays reasonably, your family responsibilities might still prevent you from taking it up. It is very difficult, not to say expensive, for wives and children to go abroad, so many players remain in England during the winter and have to find employment. Before the economic decline of the late-1980s, companies, particularly those with managing directors who were interested in sport, were prepared to employ county cricketers for six months. Many of the Sussex players, for example, used to be employed by a leading insurance company that is based in Brighton. However, such jobs are now few and far between.

Many county clubs do provide players with an income during the winter. Sussex has employed Peter Moores and Keith Greenfield over the past three years on a full-time basis, and other players part-time, to coach individuals as well as colts, club and school sides. This youth development policy, put into practice in recent years, is crucial to the future of Sussex cricket because very few children in state schools now have the opportunity to play cricket. Teachers no longer have the time to run after-hours activities like cricket; therefore, the county cricket club has had to take over the role of encouraging school children to play cricket. Sussex has paid for its county players to attend coaching courses and then used these qualified players to implement its youth policy, achieving a great deal of success. Sussex has some fine young players from state schools coming through the ranks and graduating onto the staff. At the same time, there are still ex-public schoolboy cricketers joining the staff because these schools continue to offer the facilities and the chance to play cricket most days. About 20 per cent of professional cricketers come from public schools, and I doubt whether this has significantly altered over the past twenty years. At Sussex, for example, in this year's squad, four of the staff of twenty come from public schools, the same proportion as in 1986.

Apart from the possibility of coaching, the majority of county cricketers struggle to guarantee financial security during the winter. In the past, few cricketers have had either the foresight or the money, let alone the knowledge, to set up their own businesses. The majority of county players relied on the possibility of being granted a benefit and earning a pension from the age of forty to secure their future financially. However, in years to come the guarantee of a benefit will decrease and players will have to look elsewhere for financial security.

Cricketers have become increasingly aware of the inadequacy

of their county-cricket pension. Although a professional cricketer's pension is paid out at forty, it often fails to guarantee any sort of financial security because the lump sum is based on a percentage of the player's most lucrative three years. An average pension pay-out would be between £10,000 and £20,000, which is a very poor return for someone who has played top-level sport for fifteen years. This is another area that the TCCB is investigating, and hopefully the situation will be brought into line with that of most other professional careers.

Today, more county cricketers realise not only that an alternative source of income is required for the winter, but that another career is needed to provide a living after cricket. Like myself, Jack Russell and Peter Martin have developed their talent for painting. Jack has been very successful with his artistic career and operates his own gallery, while Peter released a limited-edition print of Old Trafford last summer. I have released several limited-edition prints as well as a book, *A Cricketer's View*, illustrated with fifty-four of my paintings.

Despite the increased awareness of the need for a second career, it is still only a small percentage of professional cricketers who go to university to acquire qualifications before starting their cricket careers. However, there has been a decrease in the number of first-class cricketers coming down from Oxford and Cambridge and an increase in those arriving from the red-brick universities such as Durham, Exeter and Loughborough. Up until the late 1970s, the Oxbridge cricket teams played host to a number of first-class county cricketers such as Mike Brearley, Imran Khan, Paul Parker, Vic Marks and Peter Roebuck. More recently, only a few county cricketers have graduated from Oxford and Cambridge, Mike Atherton and John Crawley being two notable examples, while far more county cricketers have come from other universities. Over the past ten years, at least twenty graduates from Durham

University alone have played county cricket.

The reason for this shift towards players from the 'new' universities is a change in the admissions policy of Oxford and Cambridge. They are no longer prepared to accept undergraduates unless they have outstanding academic qualifications and thus those cricketers without outstanding A Level results are not accepted. As a result, the standard of the Oxbridge cricket teams is far worse today than it was twenty years ago, and it is not surprising that their first-class status is the subject of much debate.

The possession of a university degree does not, of course, guarantee a job, but for those county cricketers who do have degree-level qualifications, there should be better prospects of employment after professional cricket. Many university graduates pursue professional careers that provide high salaries and benefits, and, in light of the current economic climate and unemployment levels, it is not surprising that more recently some county cricketers have retired prematurely to pursue alternative careers. Toby Pierce, a graduate of Durham University and a Sussex county cricketer, retired at the end of the 1995 season, aged twenty-one, in order to work in the City. He was a promising opening batsman, and it can only be assumed that he felt that there were greater opportunities and a better lifestyle to be had in another career. The average salary of an uncapped first-class cricketer is low, while the lifestyle makes family life very awkward. Professional cricketers require very understanding partners. Not only are they away every other week during the summer for six days at a time, but also, when they are at home, they are playing most weekends.

Most first-class cricketers believe this situation is unlikely to change in the foreseeable future, a belief which was strengthened by a recent proposal aimed at improving the competitiveness of all eighteen county sides and the national team. It was suggested that the County Championship should be split into two leagues. Between these two leagues (a first and a second division) there would be promotion and relegation, and therefore every team, not just the top three or four, would be competitive throughout the summer. This proposal could work, but it fails to address a very important problem: county cricketers play far too much cricket and are therefore unable to produce top-quality performances all the time. The plan suggested that each county would play at least two four-day and limited-overs fixtures against every other side in its league. This would mean just as much cricket, and travelling would be just as involved, as under the current format.

England cricketers often come in for a lot of criticism, especially when compared to their Australian counterparts. The reason for England players' failure is fairly obvious to most county cricketers, but not as yet to the game's administrators. Australian state cricketers play a four-day match every other week, with time to relax, recharge their batteries and practise between matches. As a result, they are fit and keen, and this is reflected in the performances of the national side. During England's poor showing in the World Cup, many New Zealanders commented on the tired, lacklustre performances of the England team and most of the players seemed to be carrying injuries. Why do only the English players struggle with fatigue and injuries to this extent? Surely it is because they play far too much cricket. It is not surprising that some of the overseas players who play in county cricket only last for a few seasons before complaining about exhaustion and burn-out – Brian Lara and Richie Richardson being the most recent examples.

In January 1993, I played in a Shell Cup match for Wellington against Canterbury at Lancaster Park in Christchurch. Wellington successfully chased around 250 and during this innings I shared a third-wicket partnership of nearly 200 with Martin Crowe. After the game, while sitting in the changing room having a beer, Martin laughed about the madness of English county cricket. If we had been playing county cricket in England, he said, we would be packing our cricket gear, jumping into the car and driving 200 miles to our next venue, ready to play the next day.

The format of English county cricket has not really changed over the past fifty years, so why does it appear to be having such an adverse effect on the players now? Assuming that the standard of county and England cricketers has remained constant, as has the pride in playing for England, then the only answer can be the increased pressure on players to succeed. This all portrays a fairly negative view of the professional game in England and might make you wonder why anybody plays first-class cricket at all. The unglamorous answer is that the majority of players just 'fall into' the job.

Most children, particularly those who are natural ball players, play cricket because it is the summer sport. Many simply play cricket because all their friends in the football team play it. Once they have played at school or for a club's colt team, they end up playing club cricket and have trials for county under-age teams. Some progress through the county colts to the young cricketers (under 19s) and the best cricketers are given the opportunity to play county 2nd XI and then first-class cricket. It is a natural progression and very few professional cricketers can have decided at the age of eleven that they were going to play cricket for a living.

Many of those who follow cricket, let alone play as professionals, have a deep passion for the game. The thought of pursuing this passion as a job appeals to many people, but only a few succeed. For some of these few, being labelled a 'professional cricketer' is important because it makes them feel special. They like the fact that their name is in the newspaper every day and that occasionally they are recognised outside the cricket ground. I must admit I enjoyed being recognised two days after the 1993 NatWest final when my fiancée and I spent an afternoon at the Bluebell railway in Sussex. The lad serving the ice creams at the booth thanked me for my part in the final and paid for our ice creams in return for my autograph. It put smiles on our faces and I'm sure many county cricketers have enjoyed such moments.

For many cricketers, such recognition is nice but not important. More important is the thrill of succeeding, pride in their own performances, and, of course, the chance of being selected to play for England Even more important and exciting is playing in a successful team.

When Sussex defeated Northamptonshire and Glamorgan in the quarter- and semi-finals of the NatWest respectively, both against the odds, the elation at each victory, plus the thrill of knowing that we were going to play in a Lord's final, was incredible. Such experiences more than compensate for the days when nothing is going right and you don't know where the next run is coming from and or how you're going to pay the gas bill.

These brief moments of ecstasy more than make up for the times when your ambitions are frustrated. A bit like sex.

THE BIG LIE: THE ROOTS OF
THE NEW CRICKET CULTURE

6

THE ATHLETIC FALLACY
Francis Wheen

After England's mediocre showing in the 1994 Lord's Test against New Zealand, captain Mike Atherton issued a characteristically gloomy verdict, describing his team's performance as 'substandard in all departments'.

Unduly modest, I'd say. Although many of England's bowlers are trundling dullards, and our batsmen often turn out to be accident-prone prodders, we are still the undisputed world champions in one department – our ability to come up with excuses for failure.

Two years earlier, having been well and truly trounced by Pakistan (thanks largely to the devastating bowling of Wasim Akram and Waqar Younis), English players and administrators promptly accused the Pakistanis of cheating. More absurdly still, the *Cricketer* complained that the Pakistani players had sometimes drunk orange squash from bottles placed just beyond the boundary. 'Allowing the bowlers to swig away at the edge of the field cannot be conducive to the public good,' it thundered.

The winter after the Pakistani debacle, Graham Gooch led his men to India, with equally disastrous results. After the Calcutta Test, the chairman of selectors, Ted Dexter, blamed England's poor performance on air pollution and said he was commissioning a survey of smog levels in Indian cities. (The more obvious reason for defeat, the lack of variety in the English bowling attack, was not mentioned). The team's subsequent drubbing in Madras was said to be the fault of a dish of prawns that Gooch, Smith and Gatting had eaten on the eve of the match. For good measure, England's manager also grumbled that his players had been put off by the smell of the canal next to the cricket ground. At the end of the tour, after a series of inept displays by England in the one-day matches, Ted Dexter found a new excuse: his men weren't shaving often enough. 'We have to look at the whole matter of facial hair,' he announced.

By the summer of 1993, after England had failed to regain the Ashes for the second series running, Dexter had decided that supernatural forces must be at work. 'We may be in the wrong sign or something,' he said after England lost the Lord's Test. 'Venus may be in the wrong juxtaposition to somewhere else.'

The preposterous Dexter – the embodiment of the old cricketing 'gentleman' – gave way soon afterwards to the gritty Yorkshireman Ray Illingworth, an archetypal professional. But some things didn't change. Although England managed to win the first of the 1994 tests against New Zealand, it took rather longer than Illingworth would have wished. His reaction? He fired the English team's chaplain, the Rev. Andrew Wingfield-Digby, and banned the use of mobile telephones in the dressing room.

Having thus identified the cause of our feebleness on the pitch, Illingworth took his team to Lord's, but there was no discernible improvement. As England staggered towards a draw on the Monday afternoon, I waited for the inevitable apologia; and I was not disappointed. 'We didn't play well,' Mike Atherton said afterwards, 'and traditionally England haven't done well at Lord's.' Cricket, as we all know, reveres its traditions. The implication of Atherton's remark was that it would somehow have been disrespectful to his predecessors if

England had won.

Later that summer the English team put on another dismal show at Lord's, against the South Africans, and I wondered which scapegoats would be trotted out this time. The weather? The rail strike? The end of the millennium? The popularity of Nelson Mandela? As it turned out, the explanations were even more ingenious. 'Questions have been asked at Lord's these last few days to which it is hard to find reassuring answers,' John Woodcock, the reactionary doyen of cricket writers, announced in the *Times*. Such as? 'Why is DeFreitas not told it is out of order to wear a watch?' 'Why do England wear their beach clothes on the balcony?' And 'Why don't England captains shave in the morning?' Cricket conservatives seem to have a bit of a thing about razors. Have they never noticed that W. G. Grace wore a splendidly bushy beard? If it didn't do him any harm, I fail to see why a speckling of stubble should be blamed for the shortcomings of Mike Atherton or Graham Gooch.

But back to John Woodcock and his questions. 'Why', he demanded, 'is the advice of a great patriot and bowler like Alec Bedser never sought?' Although Bedser was a good bowler, his skills as an adviser are altogether more suspect. As a selector of the English team to tour Australia in 1974–5, he picked his batsmen on the assumption that they would not have to face any fast bowling. They were duly skittled out by two gents named Lillee and Thomson. His 'patriotism' is even more cranky that his sporting judgement. Bedser chaired the meeting of the English test selectors in 1968 that chose to omit Basil D'Oliveira from the English squad to tour South Africa just a few weeks after the all-rounder had scored 158 against Australia in the Oval Test. President Vorster's government had made it clear for months that it would cancel the tour rather than play against a team which included a 'coloured' man, and the decision by Bedser and his colleagues was greeted with jubilation by South African racists: the Minister of the Interior said that it was a great day for apartheid. In the 1970s, Bedser was a founding member of the National Association for Freedom, an extremely right-wing outfit which was rather keen on South Africa. Perhaps because its acronym was too embarrassingly apposite, NAFF later changed its name to the Freedom Association, but its politics remained the same.

The administrative elite of the MCC and the TCCB has long been stuffed with reactionaries like Alec Bedser, people who could never see the point of boycotting apartheid and who now speak of having 'resumed' our contests with South Africa, as if the past quarter of a century had been nothing more than a tiresome and unnecessary interruption. English cricket is, God knows, in a sorry state, but the last thing it needs is advice from flannelled fools of his kidney.

Alas, that is just what it gets; and the fools in question are as likely to be found in the cabinet room as in the committee-members' boxes at Lord's. It is no coincidence that Alec Bedser's greatest admirer – often seen sharing a joke with him at the Oval – is the Rt Hon. John Major, PC, MP. Just as the game's administrators have long treated cricket as an extension of their own brand of politics, so our political leaders like to imagine that government is merely sport by other means.

John Ruskin coined the phrase 'pathetic fallacy' to describe the Romantic poets' habit of attributing emotions to inanimate nature: happy flowers, mournful skies and so on. A related syndrome, which one might call the athletic fallacy, is the tendency to see English sporting performances as somehow symptomatic of the nation's health.

In 1993, during one of his livelier attacks on the government, the late John Smith observed that we now live in a country where even the Grand National didn't start on time. It was a joke; but I suspect that few of his listeners appreciated that. For shortly afterwards, with all due solemnity, newspaper front pages printed the findings of an inquiry into that year's aborted Grand National, presided over by a High Court judge, no less, and presented as if it were an official investigation into a serious miscarriage of justice.

Later that year, after the English football team had suffered the ultimate humiliation of being beaten by America, the *Independent* juxtaposed photographs of John Major and the then England coach Graham Taylor at the top of its front page. 'Two leaders faced their critics yesterday, determined to carry on come what may,' a headline announced. An editorial in the same day's *Sun* made the connection between sporting failure and weak government even more explicitly. 'Did you wake up with pride in your heart?' it asked. 'You probably didn't.... Whether it is football, cricket or politics, we seem to be on a losing run.... Why is Britain playing below form, why are our heads down? Because we are not being led. The British people are a great crew. What we need now is a great skipper.'

The earnest belief in sporting success as an essential precondition for political recovery is an ancient and enduring one. As Orwell commented, if it's true that the battle of Waterloo was won on the playing fields of Eton, it's equally true that every subsequent battle has been lost there. And no game lends itself more easily to analogy and metaphor than cricket, with its exotic lexicon of googlies, no-balls and sticky wickets.

In nineteenth century England, the future of the empire was often thought to depend on whether or not one could keep a straight bat; and the phrase 'It's not cricket' entered the language as a lofty put-down of those lesser breeds who refused to accept the *lex britannica* as Holy Writ. Many people over a certain age can probably still recite Sir Henry Newbolt's 'Vitai Lampada', which proceeds from a school cricket pitch ('Ten to make and the match to win') to a bloodstained battlefield, where a young officer rallies the ranks by crying 'Play up! Play up! And play the game!'

To give him his due, Newbolt was not quite as frivolous or foolish as he may sound to modern ears. What he was trying to suggest, perhaps rather clumsily, was that war should be conducted according to proper rules – a reasonably humane point of view with which no supporter of the Geneva Convention could disagree. 'War, like life itself, is a game or else a brutality worse than bestial,' he explained. 'To win a game makes the pulses leap, but not to massacre – that only chokes and disgusts.' Those who dismiss him as a bloodthirsty jingoist might be surprised by the bleakness of his other war poetry, in which ribboned coats and bumping pitches are nowhere to be seen. Here, for instance, is a verse written on Good Friday, 1915: 'Broken and pierced, hung on the bitter wire/By their most precious death the Sons of Man/Redeem for us the life of our desire –/Oh Christ how often since the world began!' He would, I suspect, have been outraged by the 'turkey shoot' on the Basra Road in the final days of the Gulf War.

No such excuses can be offered for most of his contemporaries. Although 'Vitai Lampada' is the best-known manifestation of the athletic fallacy from Victorian and Edwardian England, it was merely part of a vast literature on the subject. In 1859, a correspondent in the *Times* blamed the British Army's poor performance in the Crimea on deficiencies in the cricket system at Eton. On the outbreak of the Boer War, the Lorettonian, a public-school magazine, printed a poem 'To Loretto From Her Volunteers', which promised:

> For the bowling we are ready
> And will keep the right foot steady
> And try to not flinch as they hum past our head.

The supposed correlation between skill at games and martial prowess was still thriving at the time of the First World War, when Old Stonyhurstians in Kitchener's army were told by their school mag that 'the name of English sportsmen lies at stake'. E. W. Hornung, the creator of Raffles, extended the conceit yet further in his poem 'Lord's Leave, 1915':

> No Lord's this year: no silken lawn on which
> A dignified and dainty throng meanders.
> The schools take guard upon a fiercer pitch
> Somewhere in Flanders.
>
> Bigger the cricket here: yet some who tried
> In vain to earn a colour while at Eton
> Have found a place upon an England side
> That can't be beaten.

It reads like parody, but Hornung's intentions were wholly sincere. In later verses, the Germans are presented as demon bowlers firing their Krupp shells from 'a concrete grandstand far beyond the boundary'. Although the conditions are dreadful – 'no screen and too much mud for cricket lovers' – this is one match in which appeals against the light are not permitted.

Now that few Britons go to war, political success is measured not in military victories but in the opinion polls; and the sporting analogy has been adjusted accordingly. In 1994, a leader in the *Times* argued that the English cricketers who capitulated to the West Indies in Port of Spain had taken their cue from 'the John Major Ramblers' at Westminster. 'As Tory MPs leave for their Easter break,' the *Daily Express* editorialised, 'it is not events at Westminster they should have uppermost in their minds but those in the West Indies, where the England cricketers have just lost the test series.' With both Mike Atherton and John Major, the paper explained, it had been assumed that a change of leader would be enough to end Britain's losing streak. 'Alas, test cricket is not like that. And nor is politics.'

In a variation on the pathetic fallacy, the philosopher Gilbert Ryle invented the term 'category-mistake' for the yoking together of two incompatible concepts: 'love is a rectangle', say, or 'Thursdays are crimson'. The juxtaposition of the English cricket eleven with Her Majesty's government is undoubtedly a category-mistake; but, under the captaincy of the sports-mad John Major, it has become hard to avoid. One could even argue, only slightly fancifully, that he was propelled into Downing Street by a cricket metaphor.

In the autumn of 1990, Margaret Thatcher announced at a dinner in the City of London that she expected some fast bowling from her critics but would hit it to the boundary. Her deputy prime minister, Sir Geoffrey Howe, resigned in a huff shortly afterwards, explaining to the House of Commons that he had gone to the European wicket only to find that Mrs Thatcher had broken his bat. Howe's speech precipitated the downfall of Mrs T. and the elevation of John Major, a man who in 1956 had been named as the London *Evening Standard's* 'cricketer of the month' after taking seven wickets for Rutlish Grammar School.

A few months later, in one of her last interventions in the House of Commons, the ever-helpful Thatcher offered some free advice to her successor on how to deal with our European partners: 'In my day, government required the occasional use of the handbag. Now it will doubtless be the cricket bat and that will be a good thing because it will be harder.'

And so the metaphor became flesh. In the summer of 1995, while preparing to announce his challenge for the Tory leadership, John Redwood took himself off to Lord's to watch the West Indian batsmen in action. The following day, not to be outdone, John Major emerged from Conservative Central Office brandishing a cricket bat. He was then whisked away to Lord's. How could Redwood top that? Easy: he had himself photographed in cricket whites (which always make a man look better anyway), and let it be known that he had just returned from playing in a real game – something Major hadn't managed for several years, unless you count his brief innings in a charity match in Zimbabwe and a few balls delivered in South Africa for the benefit of the cameras. Both candidates were so keen to boast of their cricketing enthusiasm that I half-expected them to dispense with the election and settle their differences in a single-wicket contest at Lord's instead.

Major's belief in the magical potency of cricket goes way beyond the metaphorical. Inspired by his twin dreams of a classless society and a revival of competitive games in schools, the Headmaster's Conference proposed that the government should fund private education for working-class children who are good at sport, since public schools can 'foster the spirit of fair play and sportsmanship exemplified by models such as C. B. Fry, who played football and cricket for England after leaving Repton'. The public-school heads could hardly have chosen a more convincing refutation of their theory that healthy bodies make for healthy minds. Brilliant athlete though he was, Fry was also a nincompoop. In his autobiography, he paid fond tribute to the 'innate dignity' of Adolf Hitler, whom he described as a 'great man'.

The Führer was not renowned for his spirit of fair play, but nevertheless, Major and his colleagues were clearly attracted by the idea of reviving the Corinthian spirit. The sports minister Iain Sproat, who used to edit *The Cricketers' Who's Who*, has claimed that if we had more organised sport in schools 'we'd have fewer little thugs like those who murdered James Bulger', thus echoing the conclusion of the Royal Commission on Public Schools, as long ago as 1864, that 'the cricket and football fields are not merely places of exercise and amusement; they help to form some of the most valuable social qualities and manly virtues.'

This view of the game as a force for moral hegemony – devised by the upper classes of Victorian England, now perpetuated by the 'classless' John Major – is astonishingly tenacious. C. L. R. James, who as a Trinidadian Marxist might have been expected to take a radically different perspective, was utterly seduced by it: the heroes of his seminal work *Beyond a Boundary* were Thomas Arnold, the nineteenth-century headmaster of Rugby, Thomas Hughes, the author of *Tom Brown's Schooldays*, and W. G. Grace. James was dazzled by the 'grandeur' and 'moral elevation' of Arnold's ideas, apparently happy to overlook the fact that these ideas included a contempt for the working class and a terror of universal suffrage. What mattered, in C. L. R.'s view, was that Arnold introduced compulsory games for his pupils – 'the only contribution of the English educational system of the 19th century to the general educational ideas of Western civilisation'. One can almost hear John Major applauding.

Even Mike Marqusee, another expatriate Marxist, gave his book *Anyone But England* the ominous sub-title *Cricket and the National Malaise*. Thankfully, unlike James, Marqusee is not in thrall to the Victorian public-school ideology. He is scathing about the quasi-feudal system that governed cricket until well into this century, with its distinction between gentlemen and players, and its determination to perpetuate 'the myth of an enduring and natural social hierarchy'. The game's aristocratic administrators, who pretended to be guided by a sense of 'fair play', were in fact anything but fair to the working-class players whose talents they exploited. 'Pray God no professional may ever captain England,' said Lord Hawke, Yorkshire CCC's president, in 1924.

All most deplorable. Does Mike Marqusee rejoice, then, that patrician amateurs such as Hawke – who kept vulgar commerce out of cricket, or at least at a safe distance from it – have been replaced by hard-headed professionals? He does not. He winces as he surveys the present sponsor-infested game, whose Sunday League players are forced to cavort like pantaloons in garish pyjamas at the behest of AXA Equity & Law, an insurance company. White flannels 'were one of the first things that attracted me to cricket,' he reveals, 'and I mourn their loss on Sunday as much as anyone.'

Like so many cricket-loving Socialists, he is in something of a quandary. 'To the war between modernisers and traditionalists, there is no end,' he writes. 'But a socialist would be foolish to take sides in it.' This is for fear that he may find himself on the same side of the barricades as 'the crusty old traditionalists'.

Too timid, my dear fellow. Some things are true even though the *Daily Telegraph* says they are true; similarly, one should allow that some things in this country are worth conserving even though crusty old traditionalists happen to think so too. These include cricket whites, leg-spin bowling and uncovered wickets. The trouble with the Conservative Party, Evelyn Waugh used to complain, is that it has never turned the clock back by even five minutes; and he was quite right. If a Conservative government can't be bothered to save our few cherishable national institutions, like Bart's Hospital or the railway system, then what on earth is its *raison d'être*?

The same applies to the government of cricket. Although the potentates of the MCC and the TCCB are usually denounced as fossilised reactionaries, in certain important respects they aren't nearly reactionary enough. Given their hostility to almost everybody outside their own magic circle – black people, women, undeferential foreigners – one would expect them also to shun the barbarian hordes of PR consultants, marketing whiz-kids and corporate-hospitality merchants. Go to any county ground and you will see that this isn't the case. While devoting their energies to keeping women out of the Long Room at Lord's and banishing free spirits such as David Gower from the test side, the MCC and the TCCB have done nothing to prevent rich corporations from disfiguring the Arcadian scene – the boundaries, the players' shirts, the very pitches themselves – with logos and huckstering slogans. Even the umpires now wear the colours of a privatised electricity company. 'There is no doubt,' the promotions manager of the TCCB said recently, 'that it is primarily the image of the game and its track record of successful association with the business world which continue to attract corporate advertisers.'

Silly me. I thought the attractions of the game were its guile and grace, and those other qualities sketched so evocatively by Mike Marqusee: 'the arc of a straight six, the crisp, dismissive sound of a square cut, the sudden savagery of a stump uprooted by pace...the solace of an empty county ground on a bright weekday morning...the sublime waste of an entire day on something with no redeeming purpose whatsoever'.

Silly Sir Henry Newbolt, too. Had he known that the true beauty of cricket was its 'track record of successful association with the business world', he would, I feel sure, have rewritten 'Vitai Lampada' accordingly:

And it's not for the sake of a ribboned coat,
Or the selfish hope of a season's fame,
But the sponsored boots and the ten-pound note,
"Pay up! Pay up! And pay the game!"

But perhaps I'm being unfair. In their willingness to let the money-changers into the temple, the blazered buffoons at Lord's may have unwittingly proved themselves to be true traditionalists after all. Although it is tempting to see the history of English cricket as a transition from feudalism to capitalism via imperialism – without any intervening period of civilisation - the truth is more complex. Look at this cutting from the *St James's Chronicle* of 26 July 1796: 'Yesterday a cricket match was played on Hounslow Heath between the Westminster Scholars and those of Eton for 100 guineas a side, which was won by the Westminster Scholars.' So much for the equation of amateurism with the public-school spirit. A month later, the astounding sum of 1,000 guineas was put up as prize-money for a game between eleven one-legged pensioners and eleven one-armed pensioners – a stunt that even Rupert Murdoch might hesitate to repeat.

The lure of lucre spread far beyond these freakshows. In 1815, the following advertisement appeared in the *Morning Herald*: 'A grand match will be played in Lord's New Cricket Ground, St John's Wood, Marylebone, on Wednesday July 12th, and the following days, between the county of Surrey against All England, for 1,000 guineas a side.' It was only at the start of the Victorian age that this rampant commercialism, which included bets for huge stakes and plenty of skulduggery and nobbling, was extinguished. In his book *The Cricket Field*, published in 1851, the Rev. James Pycroft referred to that now-forgotten era as 'a dark chapter in the history of cricket'. Eric Parker's *History of Cricket*, written 100 years later, also described money as the 'curse' that 'blackened the game' in the early nineteenth-century. 'But', he concluded cheerfully, 'the game was greater than the curse.... Cricket was nobler than some of its players, and the straightness of it, in the balls bowled and in the bats that hit them, won in the end.'

Parker's belief that cricket's evolution ended sometime in the mid-nineteenth-century, having reached an unimprovable state of perfection, is almost touching in its imbecilic innocence; it reminds me of the final chapter of *1066 and All That*, in which 'America was thus clearly top nation and history came to an end.'

Nevertheless, Parker is half-right. Cricket may be seen as the relic of a pre-industrial age, a version of the pastoral, a colonial legacy, a continuation of the class war by other means, a gimmick for vote-hungry politicians and an alluring investment opportunity. But the game is greater than the curse, whether that curse be the oligarchs of the MCC or the predatory magnates of satellite television. George Orwell's description of England as 'a family with the wrong members in control' applies equally well to cricket: those of us who play or spectate will always find a way of preserving its subtle delights from the irresponsible uncles and bedridden aunts who seek to thwart us.

On visits to India and Sri Lanka I have often watched children hurling themselves into the game with joyous abandon, equipped with little more than a set of makeshift stumps and a dust-track wicket. These youngsters have probably never heard of Lord Hawke or Kerry Packer. What they do know is the thrill of a well-struck drive, a perfectly-pitched yorker, a soaring catch. With such pleasures still available, even to the poorest citizen, who needs metaphors?

7

THE PEOPLE'S GAME
Ian McLellan

Cricket is a game stolen from the people who devised and popularised it; it is a game controlled for nearly two hundred years by those who wanted it to become the pastime of an elite; and, finally, it is a game that has had a mostly inappropriate set of values imposed on it in an attempt to undermine its true, popular traditions. The conflict between these forces was a battle begun, not by modern cricket lovers or politically motivated outsiders, but by the people who created the game's establishment. They started the war and the arrival of the New Cricket Culture could signal the beginning of its end.

Cricket's popular tradition is directly opposed to the elite tradition of the game's establishment, which was created in the Victorian era and underpinned a class-conscious playing structure that secured the privileged position of the amateur public-school gentleman. Much was made of sportsmanship and fair play, but these were simply values borrowed and perverted from the popular tradition. The loyalties displayed within cricket's popular tradition were local patriotisms rather than those of the old school tie, and they celebrated neighbourhood and amity rather than class segregation. Cricket's ethos, the spirit of the game, evolved within this popular tradition, within the People's Game.

THE BIRTH OF THE PEOPLE'S GAME

Cricket evolved into a distinctive and refined game during the sixteenth and seventeenth centuries as part of the popular culture of south east England. These early games were festive rituals in the communal life of the parish, and there was no fast distinction between playing cricket and the sociability of the ale house, which invariably profited from the drinking and feasting that accompanied matches. The games reflected inter-village rivalries and they may have been occasioned by the 'invasion' of one parish by another. This was a common element in popular festivities and might have transformed cricket into an expression of parochial solidarity against these 'invaders'.

The game of cricket played on these occasions was never described and probably existed in several local variants. But its defining feature was a basic structure, directly inherited by modern cricket, which articulated the values of the communities that played the game. The personal confrontation between batsman and bowler expressed the individualism of village communities into which rural capitalism had already made inroads, while the team setting expressed the survival of co-operative values. The expectation that players would accept the umpire's verdict, however disappointing or unjust, reflects a society with a high level of internalised obedience to authority. The balance between individual and collectivity and the submission to rules were values of the close-knit village and, when this traditional village life was swept away towards the end of the eighteenth century, they became the values of the cricket team, outliving the rural society in which they were born.

By the beginning of the eighteenth century, cricket was already a refined game controlled by generally accepted conventions, called 'the laws' as early as 1706. These rules were probably passed on by word of mouth until aristocratic sponsors began to draw up 'Articles of Agreement'. It is here that we see the first evidence of the 'ownership' of the game being usurped. Far from introducing an 'official' set of rules for the game's own good, the main inspiration behind the 1743 creation of the 'Laws of Cricket' by the London Club was to settle betting disputes.

Large-scale betting on cricket matches, the first example of financial considerations becoming more important than the game, had been introduced some years earlier by the aristocratic descendants of those who now claim to be the defenders of cricket's 'true spirit'. As rich and powerful men, these aristocratic punters had plenty of power to influence the result of games and did so whenever they could get away with it.

Cricket, in spite of its snobbish reputation, is the only English spectator sport which is directly descended from plebeian tradition and did not originate in the public schools or university clubs. The rules of Association Football were first codified in 1843 and were based on the form of the game played by Cambridge undergraduates. The game the FA prescribed bore no resemblance to traditional folk-football, a ritualised combat involving all the young men of rival parishes which was traditionally associated with Shrove Tuesday and existed in numerous local variants. Football did not become a mass spectator sport until the 1880s, but cricket matches were regularly attracting fee-paying crowds of ten thousand by the middle of the eighteenth century. These big matches were organized by sporting aristocrats as gambling opportunities, but the competitive impetus for the vast majority of matches came from local rivalries.

In the eyes of foreign visitors, the national uniqueness of cricket was its social integration. They were struck by the flexibility and cohesion of the English social fabric and they saw this rough-and-ready social harmony reflected in cricket, which united all ranks of society in a boisterous and combative pastime. As the historian David Underdown writes, 'Even the greatest nobleman might rub shoulders on the cricket field with men of plebeian condition, as did the Dukes of Richmond and Dorset in the 1770s with the yeomen, small farmers, and artisans of the Hambledon Cricket Club.' This social mixing did not, of course, entail a levelling of class distinctions. The aristocracy expected and usually received deferential treatment on the cricket field, although the cricket writer John Nyren reveals that the excitement of matches occasionally overcame the class-conscious reflexes of the Hambledon players.

Cricketers were deferential to their aristocratic team members or opponents, but the first big cricket crowds that gathered to watch were rough, loud and disorderly. They were the same rowdy mob that attended cock-fights, boxing bouts and General Election meetings. Foreign visitors to England were shocked at the licence given to the lower orders, who seemed extraordinarily independent and outspoken.

But cricket's usurpers, the aristocrats and rich merchants, were not prepared to share the game with the riff-raff indefinitely. The creation of the world's most famous cricket club was a direct attempt to reverse cricket's tradition of social inclusion. In 1787, an aristocratic hunting and gambling set founded the Marylebone Cricket Club so that they could play on an enclosed, private ground and avoid the plebeian spectators who thronged to matches contested on common land.

Aristocratic patronage of cricket was a smokescreen for the decay of rural paternalism in the second half of the eighteenth century. Wealthy landowners were adamant that if agricultural improvement dictated enclosing or interfering with customary rights, it would have to be done. In many cases this involved destroying villagers' access to the commons on which games of cricket had traditionally been held. The modern image of the English countryside, a patchwork of meadow and hedgerow, is a creation of enclosing and market-oriented farming. The semi-mythical 'village green', popularised by cricket writers like Edmund Blunden as the cradle of cricket, is an extension of the scenery that was shaped in this period by the forces of agricultural capitalism, the same forces which transformed the ancient village life that was really responsible for the birth of cricket.

The disruptive impact of capitalism on traditional rural life is illustrated by the financial straits of the great Kent cricketer Alfred Mynn, the embodiment of the English yeoman of rural legend who trained on beef and beer. On more than one occasion Mynn was imprisoned for debt and bailed out by his friends on the eve of a great match. The old festive customs were still full of vitality in the nineteenth century, but they were broken up once and for all by the great agricultural depression of 1870–95. The complex feelings associated with the pastoral nature of cricket, the mood of melancholy longing for a halcyon rural life that never really existed, were produced by this transformation of rural society and the identification of village cricket with an idyllically stable community which has vanished.

The Game Is Hijacked

The MCC began to take on the governance of the game in the 1820s. It dedicated its energies to promoting the cricket played by a privileged minority and opposing the technical advances made by professional bowlers. It frustrated liberal followers of the game to such an extent that in 1864 the *Sporting Life* led a campaign for a 'cricket parliament'.

The task of popularising the game fell to William Clarke's professional All-England XI (1846–70) which toured the provincial towns and emerging industrial cities playing against local teams of twenty or twenty-two. Professional sides (which consisted mainly of working-class men, the upper classes playing only as amateurs) also established cricket's popularity within the Empire, embarking on the first overseas tours. The cricketers in the All-England XI, and the rival United England XI, were nearly all from skilled trades, and they believed in individualism, self-respect and self-reliance, the values of the 'aristocracy of labour' that dominated mid-Victorian working-class politics. But cricket was a precarious profession, limited to the prime of life, and several cricketers at the end of their working days were faced with the dilemma of 'the workhouse or the river'.

The professionals dominated mid-Victorian cricket but their influence began to decline in the 1860s. Rifts within the professional ranks and the growing popularity of county cricket led to the break-up of the professional elevens. Moreover, the MCC began to use its authority to usurp the independence and freedom of contract of the professionals, introducing playing qualifications which curtailed their bargaining power by restricting their mobility of labour. The county clubs which mushroomed in late-Victorian England treated their professionals as the hired servants of gentlemen subscribers, and county committees enforced the strictest standards of deference, discipline and loyalty.

The push to put the professionals in their place was accompanied by the transformation of cricket from an outdoor exercise or amusement into a symbol of the privileged code of ethics of the English gentleman. This transformation occurred in the public schools, where there was a belief that the lessons of team spirit, leadership and self-reliance taught on the cricket field prepared boys for a life of public service. Before the rise of the public schools, early 'gentlemen' cricketers were a motley collection of yeomen, merchants, clergymen, solicitors, squires, rakes and peers. The class-conscious sense of identity produced by a public-school education replaced this flexible definition of a gentleman cricketer with a consuming obsession with the distinction between amateur and professional. This obsession had nothing to do with whether or not you pursued cricket for your livelihood, but it did enforce a rigid class separation in the game, upheld by innumerable petty insults and inequalities which included different dressing-rooms, different entrances onto the playing arena and different forms of address.

The public-school gentleman was stamped with an effortless social superiority and style which became the hallmark of the amateur batsmen of the Golden Age. If their batting savoured of a lordly superiority, so did their captaincy. Joe Darling, the Australian captain, remembered hearing 'some English captains speak to their professionals like dogs...no Australian would stand it for one moment'. Cricket ought to be a well-mannered game, but, a hundred years before sledging, the feelings of class contempt harboured by amateur public-school gentlemen made a mockery of this image. Cricket's grandees, among them Sir Pelham Warner and Lord Hawke, were quick to paint professionals who questioned amateur leadership or the convention of the amateur skipper as 'mischief-makers who seem bent on creating a class warfare in the cricket world'. But it was the amateur public-school gentleman, with his brightly coloured blazer and cap, and his superior attitude, who was really responsible for introducing class feeling into cricket.

At the end of the century – when the cult of games was at its most exotic – the public schools were increasingly providing men to run an empire, and cricket came to be seen as a training ground for an imperial vocation. The apotheosis of cricket as a great imperial project knitting together the different peoples of the Empire was at odds with the game's racial segregation in the Raj and elsewhere. Nevertheless, cricket's association with the

Empire did rescue the sport from insular English xenophobia. The Empire scattered the English governing class across the globe and the amateur cricketers of the early twentieth century, many of whom were born in colonial possessions, combined the confident identity of the English public-school gentlemen with an outlook on life broadened by exposure to different cultures. Douglas Jardine, the Harelquins-capped strategist of 'bodyline', contemptuously rejected Christianity as 'rewards and fairies' and searched for spiritual meaning in an understanding of Hindu philosophy.

CRICKET'S POPULAR REVOLUTION
The organization of cricket through an increasingly formalised County Championship created the competitive structure which enabled the game to develop as a modern spectator sport. Popular opinion was responsible for the formation of the County Championship, a development resisted by the authorities at Lord's, who feared that the identification of first-class cricket with county cricket would detract from the prestige of matches played between amateurs and professionals at Lord's or on country-house weekends. A *Times* editorial in 1887 explained that 'always popular, cricket has become vastly more popularised during the last twenty years. The impetus to the game has made competition keener and has produced something of a mania within the sporting press (who decided the county champion until 1894) for canvassing 'results' of county cricket during each season.'

The Hon R.H. Lyttelton, writing in 1898, believed that the promotion of first-class cricket as an entertainment for the gate-paying spectator was a betrayal of the amateur cricketer and his ethos that the game should be played for the game's sake. He linked the decline of the amateur to the growth of commercialism exactly as former *Wisden Almanack* editor

Graeme Wright did, one hundred years later, in his book *Betrayal: The Struggle for Cricket's Soul*. Lyttelton argued:

> It is an unfortunate fact that the tendency of first-class cricket nowadays is to swamp the amateur by the professional. Some of our best county teams are almost wholly composed of the latter class.... What has happened in consequence? Cricket – i.e. first-class cricket – is becoming a regular monetary speculation. Thousands upon thousands troop almost daily to see the big matches, flooding the coffers of the county or club, which does its very best to spin out the match for the sake of the money. If this continues, our best matches will become nothing better than gate money contests, to the detriment of the true interests of the game and its lovers.

Lyttelton's view that the County Championship has transformed first-class cricket into a business enterprise, with profit as its main aim, is shared by E. V. Lucas, who wrote in the *Times* in 1908 that:

> A hard utilitarianism and commercialism have far too long controlled [English cricket]; and the new conditions of the game as a spectacle with a sufficiency of stars, have made it necessary that the principal participants in the first-class game to-day should be prepared to give so much time to it as practically to be debarred from any other occupation – thus converting what began as an occasional pastime, marked by geniality and rapture, into a more or less mechanical trade. The forces of industrialisation have mechanised and commercialised a sporting pastime, removing its appeal to sentiment and the imagination, and these forces are embodied by the professional who pursues cricket as a trade and plays with a mechanical efficiency.

Lyttelton's fears about the swamping of amateurs and Lucas's dismay at cricket's conversion into a 'mechanical trade' express the alarm of the game's traditional masters at the changing image of cricket from an aristocratic pastime into a form of popular entertainment. Looking back, the Golden Age appears to have been dominated by the opulent talents of amateur batsmen, but in the eyes of reactionaries like Lyttelton and Lucas it was the dawn of 'professional mechanism'.

The great urban crowds drawn to first-class cricket matches in the last quarter of the nineteenth century resist any simple explanation. The growing prosperity of the working-class meant that they were able to spend money on leisure activities for the first time. But why did the working man choose to spend his money at cricket? The key to this puzzle is the historical experience of urbanisation. The Victorian urban working class were immigrants from the countryside, or the descendants of immigrants, drawn to the cities by the demands of factories for labour. They were attracted to cricket matches by nostalgia for the rural existence they had left behind, its hardships trans-figured by distance. In the timelessness of a game played over three days, its ritualised pattern, the community spirit and the individuality of the players, they found an escape from the crowded anonymity of the city and the mechanical routine of factory work into an imagined pre-industrial order.

Working-class spectators brought to matches the standards of behaviour of a highly disciplined workforce. Nevertheless, they overstepped what the game's self-appointed guardians considered acceptable conduct by loudly criticising players and shouting against slow play. Despite recent controversy over the Barmy Army's chants and songs, there is nothing new in the allegation that the polite, decorous world of cricket is being contaminated by rowdy football hooligans. In 1913, E.H.D. Sewell blamed the press for 'endeavouring to encourage the football element among spectators at our cricket crowds'.

Cricket writer Roy Peskety wrongly asserts that 'Until the West Indians from Brixton and other London surrounds brought their lively Calypso music and the insidious rhythm of rattled Coca-Cola tins to Lord's it was almost a sin to make a noise during a game of England's national sport: cricket.' True, cricket in the 1930s, 1940s and 1950s was watched in hushed silence, interspersed with polite applause, but this was certainly not the case before the First World War. Modern standards of crowd behaviour represent a return to the boisterous atmosphere of the 1890s and 1900s rather than any catastrophic break with the past. If you want to imagine what it must have been like watching a match from the cheap seats when Barnes was bowling to Trumper, Spofforth to Grace, or Mynn to Parr, go and stand next to the Barmy Army and sing along.

Popular interest in cricket boomed in the 1920s: its coverage expanded in the national press, ball-by-ball commentaries were broadcast on the radio, and the cricketers pictured on cigarette cards were the most famous sporting celebrities of the day. The First World War had destroyed the frivolous and extravagant society of upper-class Edwardian England and, with it, the artificial idyll of country-house cricket. Alec Waugh, writing in 1922 (already an egregious snob at the age of twenty-four), was saddened 'to think how quickly that world has passed, and how effectively the machinery of our industrial system has already taken cricket for itself. Nyren's game is no longer entertained for a few. It has become a part of the national life, and probably, if the Bolsheviks get their way with her, it will be nationalised with the cinema and the theatre and Association Football.' (The Bolsheviks are still trying to take cricket over: Mike Marqusee's remedy for the malaise of English cricket is nationalisation.)

The populist image of cricket in the 1930s may explain why

English fascism, which was largely confined to the upper classes, became associated with rugby rather than cricket. The military values that were influential among the aristocracy, in the public schools and on the radical right held no appeal for the cloth-capped workers and lower middle-class suburbanites who flocked to cricket between the wars. According to George Orwell, the Nazis systematically suppressed cricket, 'which had gained a foothold in Germany before and after' the First World War. The game was seen as anti-Fascist in spite of ex-England captain C.B. Fry's attempts to convince Nazi youth leaders that cricket was the key to producing model Nazi citizens.

THE PEOPLE'S GAME RECLAIMED

Attendances boomed at first-class matches after the Second World War, temporarily reversing the waning of interest in county cricket during the 1930s. But crowds began to decline steeply in the mid 1950s and county cricket lost its *raison d'être* as a spectator sport. From a historical perspective, first-class cricket's decline has been constant since attendances began to fall off prior to the First World War, with intervals of renewed enthusiasm in the 1920s and 1940s. For over ninety years the vast majority of spectators have voted first-class cricket dull.

Cricket's decline is paralleled by the rise and ascendancy of football. Eric Midwinter pinpoints the 'switch-over juncture' from cricket to football at around 1900, when the numbers 'watching first-class cricket, destined to decline substantially, and League football, on the verge of rising mightily, were much the same'. Soon after 1900, once the grandeur of the Golden Age had faded, football came to be seen as a threat to the very existence of county cricket. According to F.B. Wilson, writing in the *Times* in 1914, 'This season sees county cricket trembling in the balance, for without popular support it must die.

Undoubtedly, Association Football has hurt county cricket.'
Wilson's explanation for the popularity of football is the
modern age's demand for instant results – 'People in these
mercantile days want a big return for their money' – exactly the
same explanation that is now advanced for the popularity of
one-day cricket.

Surely it is time for traditional cricket to accept that we live in
'mercantile days'. The creation of a game that only appeals to
people with an informed understanding of its subtleties, skills
and tactics defies the object of a spectator sport, which is to be
spectacular. Modern one-day cricket, played in the adventurous manner of Sri Lanka, is the spectacular game that
cricket used to be, and if traditional, first-class cricket were
played in the same spirit it would attract the crowds back to the
game.

The arena of play is only part of the spectacle of a sporting
occasion, the crowd is equally important, but cricket's administrators have made few attempts to reach a new, broader
audience for the game. Cricket's leadership has been stripped of
its veneer of paternalism, but its instincts are still anti-populist
and exclusive, a fact revealed by the new kind of crowd segregation introduced by the growth of corporate hospitality.
Cricket's establishment has ensured that cricket has not
become the national game of a multi-cultural nation by
pursuing a ticket-sales policy that effectively discriminates
against those from ethnic minorities, stamping down on the
more boisterous behaviour of fans and doing little to encourage
the natural interest in cricket within the UK's Pakistani, Indian
and Caribbean communities.

After England's drubbing by the West Indies in 1976, even the
reactionary Robin Marlar was smart enough to spot that the
shared, joyous celebration of their team by West Indian
supporters had revolutionised cricket into a vital outlet for

pent-up emotions which could have been released in disorder and riot. In the most unexpected way, that West Indian tour of England reaffirmed the virtues of cricket as a socially integrative game. But musical instruments were banned from cricket grounds in the 1980s, driving away West Indian supporters who attended test matches to participate in a festive occasion, and now test crowds in a West Indian year are almost exclusively white.

The prevailing sense of cultural malaise in the late 1980s encouraged the view that the listless performances of the English cricket team were symptomatic of a national crisis of identity. In fact, anxieties about national decline have attached themselves to cricket from the 1890s, if not before. It is a myth that the years of cricket's Golden Age were imbued with a national mood of complacent self-assurance. The poor quality of recruits in the Boer War led many in the opinion-forming classes to believe that living conditions in the industrial cities – overcrowding, malnutrition, disease – had degenerated the nation's stock of manpower, and throughout the Edwardian period Ashes victories were received as heartening news that the nation could still produce resourceful, active young men.

But the great English cricketers of the Edwardian period were simply products of a strong domestic first-class game. Likewise, the lacklustre performances of today's English cricket team can be blamed largely on the ailing county game.

The difference in approach and style between eye-catching amateur and expert professional made possible the finest moments of English cricket in the Golden Age, but it is also responsible for the drabness of much of English cricket. Teams from other countries have been able to combine adventure and expertise, but this has proved impossible in England because of the historic amateur/professional split.

In 1963, amateur status was abolished, acknowledging a fact

already accomplished by social and economic change. Amateur and professional developed together; accordingly, the disappearance of amateurism was accompanied by the decline of professionalism. English professionals, despite the huge number of games they play each year, are now the most amateur of all first-class cricketers. Peter Roebuck confessed in 1984 that county cricketers 'do very little repetitive practice designed to master our craft. In fact, most of us were technically better at 14 than we are now.' So much for the great school of professional batsmen, for Arthur Shrewsbury, Jack Hobbs and Len Hutton, who tirelessly worked at their game in the nets to refine already consummate techniques. The modern professional ethos of getting by in spite of a faulty technique and hanging on to a team place can only be destroyed by making cricket an open, semi-professional game. But this does not mean the return of the moneyed amateur, selected to play for his county because of social status and enhanced coaching opportunities.

Dennis Silk, the chairman of the Test and County Cricket Board, commented after England's crushing defeat by Sri Lanka in the World Cup quarter-final that 'If our team keeps going the way it has been going, then our game will die. All you will have left will be village and club cricket.'

The game's leadership discouraged the growth of test cricket in the late-Victorian period precisely because it threatened to overshadow an elitist form of club cricket, and also because the Australian cricketers were not gentlemen but enjoyed amateur status, a subversive violation of cricket's class structure. Now, it appears, test cricket is all that matters, and village and club cricket are, at most, a backwater. Silk's warning was intended to raise alarm that English cricket could soon be finished, but it also grudgingly acknowledges that cricket will never die in the villages and clubs in which it was born and nourished.

The story of cricket is the most incredible in sport. A game that began as a festive custom of the pre-capitalist Kentish village has become one of the great commercial sports of the southern hemisphere, and the sporting religion of Southeast Asia, forging the national identities of new nation-states. This massive shift in cricket's world order has underlined just how the game's culture is changing. But many of cricket's supposedly hallowed traditions were concocted in the late-Victorian period to support amateur-dominated institutions. No one should mourn their passing. Cricket's fund of common values are descended from the traditional festive culture of the mass of ordinary people who follow the game. As long as these values retain their symbolic importance in everyday emotional life, then cricket will continue to reflect them and it will remain the People's Game.

BRAVE NEW BALL GAME:
MONEY AND MEDIA

8

THE SKY'S THE LIMIT
David Cohen

'Money? We don't really talk about money.' This reluctance, paranoia even, within the cricketing establishment when it comes to talking about finance is part and parcel of an antiquated notion that the intrusion of commerce into the game will sully its integrity. Yet with the signing by the Test and County Cricket Board of a £58 million television deal with BSkyB and the BBC in the summer of 1994, professional cricket has undoubtedly entered the commercial age. The national game may not command the riches enjoyed by football, but there is much more money flowing into the coffers than there was even three years ago.

Just how rich is English cricket? Where is the new money coming from? How are the spoils shared out amongst the counties? And how much is trickling down to the players? Neither the pundits nor the insiders have developed an accurate picture of how much money is sloshing around the cricket world. Or, more alarmingly, a coherent plan of what to do with it. More than any other aspect of the game, the burgeoning financial base of the New Cricket Culture is an untold story.

The man with the answers to the key questions is Cliff Barker, a chartered accountant who heads the finance committee at the TCCB, but initially, like the spokesman of a secret society, he is reluctant to talk. 'The TCCB is an employers' association, not a limited company,' he explains, 'and therefore has no obligation to make its income and expenditure public knowledge.' Rather than filing annual accounts at Companies House, where they may be publicly analysed and scrutinised, it turns out that the TCCB are accountable only to their twenty members: the eighteen first-class counties, the MCC and the Minor Counties Cricket Association. The most an intrepid outsider can hope for is an abbreviated version of the TCCB's audited annual return, which is available from an obscure London-based government department called the Certification Office for Trade Unions and Employers' Associations.

'For a number of reasons, the detailed information we prepare is for members' eyes only,' insists Barker. What reasons might they be? 'Sound commercial ones. We're in a competitive situation with overseas cricket boards of control. Anyhow, it's not in cricket's interests to appear as if we're awash with cash. It may deter some people from putting money into the grassroots development of the sport,' he says.

In what way are the TCCB and the Australian Cricket Board financial competitors? It's a lame excuse and Barker knows it.

The public perception is that cricket is still largely run by amateurs. From county level to the international game, there appear to be few full-time administrators – men who make a living from running the game – and even fewer skilled in financial management. The worry persists: Is cricket equipped to handle efficiently the large amounts of money that are flowing in? Even among the more conservative commentators there is a recognition that things must change. *Daily Telegraph* cricket correspondent Christopher Martin-Jenkins is already on record demanding that the TCCB become more accountable. 'They should be obliged to publish and justify their income and expenditure. The board needs to become more like ICI and less like MI5,' he says.

After a lengthy argument, Barker does express some sympathy with the view that the TCCB needs to become more financially accountable. Indeed, he admits that there are plans afoot to move in that direction. As a compromise he is prepared to give 'a broad breakdown' of the TCCB's income and expenditure. The figures make for interesting reading.

In 1995, the total income of the TCCB amounted to £30 million. This income comprised: £12 million television revenue; £9m commercial sponsorship and perimeter advertising; £6 million match surpluses (ticket sales for test matches, limited-overs internationals and the one-day domestic competitions, less the cost of staging such matches); and £3 million merchandising and sundry income. That represents a 40 per cent hike on the previous year's total income of £21.5 million and a doubling of the 1991 income of £14.6 million. Receipts from ticket sales have risen only marginally in the last four years, but in that time the money coming into professional cricket has doubled.

The main reason for the prodigious rise in revenue is, of course, the much-hyped 1994 television contract with BSkyB and the BBC. It was the first time the TCCB had put the television rights out to competitive tender – previously the BBC had sole rights – and the result was a vastly improved £58 million deal for cricket (payable over four years), which supplanted the previous three-year contract of £15 million. So whereas the TCCB received only £5 million from the BBC in 1994, television revenue in 1995 jumped to £12 million. That figure is set to rise still further to £15 million a year over the remaining three years of the TV deal, translating to a cool £10 million a year extra for cricket.

Add to this the increased rates being squeezed out of commercial sponsors like Cornhill and Benson & Hedges by the TCCB for the right to have their names associated with the national game – annual commercial sponsorship has risen by 80 per cent in four years from £5 million to £9 million – and one gets a sniff of just how profitable cricket has become.

A tranche of the new money – £1.9 million in year one and £9.5 million in total over four years – has been set aside for 'grass-roots development' of the sport and earmarked for the recently formed Cricket Foundation amidst much pre-publicity. The problem is that 'grass-roots' is a catch-all term and no one is yet precisely clear what it means. Will the money go to schools? Will it fund community projects? Or will it go to fostering young talent at academies of excellence? If so will the academies be run by the counties or will there be a national academy of the sort so admired in Australia?

But grass-roots money aside, who are the beneficiaries? The function of the TCCB is to act as a clearing house. So, after deducting the salaries of their twenty-five full-time professional staff, the costs of running the English test side and numerous other expenses, the entire balance is distributed more or less equally to the member counties. The whole structure of the TCCB has been widely criticised as giving too much power to the counties, so the fact that they have allocated themselves the lion's share of the new money must come as no surprise. In 1995, the distribution to the counties was £15 million, double that of 1990. Each county received a basic £750,000, rising to £900,000 in 1996, with bonus amounts paid to counties hosting test matches and according to success in domestic competitions. This equal method of disbursement ensures that the new money will not widen the gap between rich and poor counties. Indeed, if anything, the financial prospects of even the least competitive ounties have never been rosier.

But little of this windfall of millions has trickled down to the players. According to Middlesex and former England captain Mike Gatting, the top test players in the richest counties are paid a basic salary of between £25,000 and £35,000 a year. By comparison, Manchester United's Eric Cantona is reported to be on £20,000 a week. 'The disparity,' says Gatting, 'means that when you talk to kids about whether they prefer to play cricket or football, there is no contest.'

John Holmes, who is agent to Michael Atherton, Dominic Cork and formerly David Gower, says that the money the top players earn from their counties is so pitiful that it's not worth negotiating about. 'As an agent I don't even bother with the counties,' he says. 'It is only through personal sponsorships and endorsements that test players can gross real money – more than £100,000 a year – but even that is nothing compared to big stars in other sports or even top cricketers in other countries.' Sachin Tendulkar, for example, recently signed a sponsorship deal worth around £7 million and both Shane Warne and Brian Lara have become millionaires.

Holmes continues: 'The whole structure of cricket in this country needs to be rethought. It was set up by a bunch of terribly nice chaps when Queen Victoria was on the throne. They're still nice chaps, but they're out of touch: a county championship of eighteen mediocre teams, where most games are played before three men and a dog, is not on. When is the last time anyone heard the county championship being discussed in the pub? It doesn't enter the public consciousness. There needs to be a premier league with eight excellent, competitive teams which people want to watch. It needs to become a television spectacle. Only then can professional cricketers hope to be properly paid.'

But for now most of the 400 county players have to rely on the minimum wage hammered out on their behalf by the players' union, the Professional Cricketers' Association (PCA). In 1995, the minimum wage for a capped player stood at a paltry £14,500 a year. For the previous five years, it had bumped along with tiny annual increases of roughly the rate of inflation (5 per cent), whereas total county revenue, comprising the aforementioned TCCB distribution as well as their own negotiated commercial sponsorship, had risen by 100 per cent.

It was a ludicrous, exploitative state of affairs. Unlike the situation in South Africa and Australia, where many professional cricketers have second careers, English cricketers are full time. They devote their peak earning years to the counties, yet by the time they retire from cricket they have little to show for it financially and no alternative career to fall back on. They may make a little extra money from coaching and media work in the off-season, and look forward to a benefit after ten capped years, but by and large they are reliant on their county salaries. For most, this does not rise significantly above the minimum wage.

In an attempt to get something for the players out of the millions that the TCCB and the counties are making from the TV companies, the PCA abandoned their softly, softly approach and appointed their first full-time general secretary, David Graveney. His brief was to take a more aggressive negotiating position with the TCCB. The result was a £4,000 rise in the minimum wage of capped players to £18,500 for the 1996 season.

Graveney hailed this as a major success. But the reality is that Graveney's PCA is still a toothless tiger. They receive almost all their £100,000 funding from the TCCB. They have no independence and hence no real power. As Graveney admits, 'We went in demanding a £20,000 minimum wage. The TCCB offered £18,500. And we said okay. We were not in a position to argue. The players could consider strike action, but that has never been seriously contemplated and we are not that way inclined.'

The problem for professional players is compounded by the fact that the attitude of their employers, the counties, often seems stuck in the mid-1950s. Gwyn Stone, secretary of Glamorgan County Cricket Club, for example, considers that the average professional cricketer should feel 'lucky' if he earns more than £20,000 a year. 'How can I put it?' he says. 'He's doing something he enjoys. A lot of people would give their right arm to be a county cricketer.' That might be true. But a lot of people would give their right arm to be a professional golfer, footballer or tennis player, yet no one in their right mind (who lives in the 1990s) would dare suggest that they be paid peanuts because 'they enjoy what they do'. Gwyn Stone, like many county paymasters, is out of touch with the modern game.

Cricketers at Surrey, one of the richest counties, fare little better. According to Paul Sheldon, Surrey chief executive, their cricketers are paid an average of £20,000 a year. The total Surrey wage bill in 1994 comprised a mere 20 per cent of the total county revenue of £3.8 million. It's almost as if the players are incidental. Compare this state of affairs to football, where players' wages of £140 million absorb 80 per cent of gate receipts and 55 per cent of total turnover. The relative value of cricketers and footballers to their respective employers becomes starkly apparent.

'The truth is that our cricketers are not very good and they get paid accordingly,' says Sheldon. 'The issue in cricket today is not remotely about money. In fact, you could argue that the new money will merely obfuscate the issue. What we need is the right structure – like a two-division championship – for the long-term development of the game. Unfortunately, the TCCB is too unwieldy to bring it about. The member counties vote for their own parochial interests and few are able to make decisions in the best interests of the game.'

The clamour for a more competitive two-division championship with a premier league has recently received the public support of TCCB chairman Dennis Silk. But, as Sheldon suggests, it will be a tough job convincing the lesser counties, who are unlikely to vote themselves into the obscurity of a second division. If a premier league were to become a reality, it might be the cue for a football-like transfer system to be introduced to the game. More than £100 million was spent on player transfers among the ninety-two football league clubs in 1994/5.

What effect would such a revolutionary move have on cricket? 'Transfer fees would bust the game,' opines Graveney. 'Despite being wealthier than ever before, no county could afford it. Cricket is a funny old game. It is followed by millions and watched by very few. Take Somerset for example – approximately 43,000 people paid to watch them over the whole of the 1995 County Championship season. That's less than the attendance at one Manchester United football match.' Perhaps a scaled-down transfer fee system could work in the context of a more competitive and popular premier league. But, until then, any discussion of transfer fees must be regarded as premature.

A voice that has hitherto remained silent in the debate on the future shape of cricket has been that of the commercial sponsors. Second only to the television companies, their cheques comprise a major slice of the new money. For example, Cornhill Insurance, the test match backers and probably the biggest sponsors of English cricket, doubled their contribution from £1.1 million in 1992 to £2.3 million in 1996. Britannic Assurance pay a not insubstantial £1.65 million over three years for the right to have their name pinned to the rather pedestrian County Championship.

What do sponsors want for their money? And is cricket delivering? On the record, most major sponsors pronounce that being associated with the national sport does 'no end of good for their image', that they're 'quite happy' with the value that they're getting and that they 'have no wish to get involved in the running of the game'. Off the record, they express some concern as to whether the marketing committee of the TCCB is up to the job. With all the counties looking out for their own interests, it's too unwieldy to be a really effective organisation, they say.

So far, the TCCB has yet to plunge its commercial sponsors into the cut and thrust of the sort of competitive tendering that has brought such vast riches from the sale of television rights. Nevertheless, Geoff Mayhew, publicity manager for Cornhill Insurance, concedes that the TCCB is a much more formidable opponent than it used to be. 'The TCCB negotiation used to be run by people who were there to administrate the game rather than market it. They have a professional marketing set-up now. They've started to bring themselves into the modern world, which is a good thing because they're trying to understand the needs of sponsors and to deliver.'

But not all the sponsors are happy. Whittingdales, the financial services company, which bankrolled the coaching and development of the England squad to the tune of £1 million over four years, withdrew their sponsorship in a blaze of publicity. Unlike sponsors whose main motivation is cold commercial logic, Whittingdale's interest always derived from the fact that their managing director, Patrick Whittingdale, is an incurable enthusiast. 'I gave the money because I wanted England to start winning again,' he says. 'I wanted my money to be used to employ a sports psychologist, a nutritionist and to provide the kind of back-up that Bob Woolmer has set up in South Africa. But the England management resisted and resisted. It was in the Whittingdale budget, for example, that the England management would fly to Florida, USA to see how a winning baseball team is prepared. They never went. There is zero preparation of the mind in the English team. They don't want to change. Consequently, they didn't really know what to do with my money.'

When David Gower was interviewed after England's dismal performance in the 1996 World Cup, his remedy for improvement was exactly the same as that of Whittingdale. 'What England need,' reflected Gower, 'is a sports psychologist, a nutritionist and to provide the sort of back-up that Bob Woolmer has put in place in South Africa.' In this country at least, Whittingdale appears to be a man ahead of his time.

Finally, what impact has the National Lottery had on the game's finances? Recent applications for lottery money, totalling an estimated £30 million, by Surrey, Durham, Hampshire and the MCC to redevelop their grounds and increase spectator capacity were deferred by the Sports Council on the damning grounds that 'there is no overall structure or plan within cricket'. Derek Casey, chief executive of the Sports Council, which administers the Lottery Sports Fund, delivered a harsh attack on the way the game is run in this country. He also questioned the popularity of county cricket. 'The number of events requiring increased spectator accommodation must be limited,' he said. 'We do not believe that funding these schemes for increased seating (when the grounds are only full on a handful of days each year) is the best way of boosting cricket at all levels.'

Decisions like these, which hit the counties where it hurts most – in their pocket – may provoke the administrators of the game to drag themselves (without too much kicking and screaming) into the twenty-first century. What is needed are bold steps to make the domestic game more competitive and exciting. And a realisation that cricket needs more commercialism, not less, to take it into the next century. The money and the success will follow.

If that offends the purists, so be it.

9

CRICKET 2000: HOW THE MEDIA
REINVENTED THE GAME
Jim Melly

Of all the forces that have shaped the New Cricket Culture, the media has been the most powerful. The relationship between cricket and the media grows ever closer and no part of the game is left untouched by its influence. From the money injected into the game to the new fans brought in as a result of increased coverage, television has been the main inspiration behind the modernisation of cricket. The press – both tabloid and broadsheet – has played its part in transforming the public's perception of the game in response to the changing agenda set by television.

But even this is to undersell the influence of the media on the game. Here, at the end of the twentieth century, cricket coverage, especially on television, has actually become part of the game itself. It is now potentially as big an influence on the course of a player's career or the result of a match or series as any Brian Lara or Shane Warne; as important to the shape of the domestic and international game as any administrative body, whether the ultra-traditional MCC or the more modern (in sporting terms at least) International Cricket Council.

We live in the 'information age', an era which is defined by the media and to which sport has had to adapt accordingly. Television coverage of football, tennis and other sports has been improved by the development of broadcast technology and techniques. However, the game that has adapted best to the television age has been cricket. We have entered the era of Cricket TV.

Only cricket has clasped the cameras to its bosom to the extent of incorporating television into the game. The technical advances made by broadcasters since the early 1980s – stump cameras, wicket microphones and side-on views of run-outs and stumpings – have been dramatic. Many of these innovations have their roots in a minor cricket television revolution that took place some twenty years ago: World Series Cricket.

The knock-on effects of Kerry Packer's World Series Cricket in Australia during the 1970s cannot be overestimated. Keith MacKenzie, the BBC TV executive producer responsible for cricket, has nothing but respect for Channel 9 (Packer's TV network). 'Suddenly, not only did the way cricket was played and marketed change, but also the way it was televised,' says MacKenzie of World Series Cricket. 'What he [Kerry Packer] was trying to do was to get both a new spectator audience and a new television audience, so they did things dramatically differently.'

Initially, this meant simple things like double-ended coverage, originally introduced by Packer because he was bored of spending half the day 'looking at batsmen's arses'. It may seem laughable now, but this innovation caused a huge stir when it was first introduced in Britain. Other changes, such as a side-on view of stumpings and run-outs, and even the electronic on-screen scorecards, were first used by Channel 9.

But Packer realised that all the technical gadgetry and televisual effects in the world couldn't provide that other component required by great television sport: atmosphere. As with football, the paying punters are an integral part of the experience of cricket. Packer realised this and day/night matches, perhaps the most potent and exciting symbol of cricket's absorption into television (and vice versa), drew in a whole new audience.

The history of cricket coverage in Britain has been much more mundane. Until the end of the 1980s, BBC TV carried the only test cricket coverage in the UK. Both the conservatism of BBC management (regarding spending and format) and that of the cricket authorities meant that any progress made by BBC cricket producers was bound to be slow. In January 1990, starting with the tour of the West Indies, BSkyB began live broadcasts of England's overseas tests. As they drew on coverage supplied by the host nation's broadcaster, BSkyB did not have the problems faced by the BBC regarding either cost of production or pedestrian cricket authorities.

The television coverage of cricket has become more than just the presentation of cricket matches. The line between reporting cricket and becoming part of the game was finally crossed with the introduction of the third umpire. As well as the two umpires present on the field of play, test matches now have a third, armed with a television screen. He can call on TV replays of the relevant action, adjudicate run-outs, stumpings and boundaries. In no other sport (apart from a brief experiment in american football's NFL) has television been brought into the confines of a game.

Cricket TV doesn't just report the news: Cricket TV is the news.

Cricket TV has introduced an entirely new experience to cricket fans. In the past, players were observed from the boundary, the distance a shield from the public. Cricket TV leaves no hiding place for players: their every glance and glare held in close-up, their emotions laid bare. Curtly Ambrose's demolition of England in Port-of-Spain during the 1994 test series, his confrontation with Steve Waugh a year later (when Curtly was practically pulled off Waugh by captain Richie

Richardson) and Dominic Cork's hat trick at Old Trafford are all examples of how Cricket TV adds to the drama of the game for the viewer. But more than this, Cricket TV can actually influence matches themselves, and the cricket authorities have had to learn to deal with the new environment that Cricket TV has created.

A prime example of this occurred during the fifth test between South Africa and England in January 1996. The TV cameras clearly showed England batsman Graham Thorpe run out. Neither of the on-field umpires asked for the third umpire's decision and Thorpe was ruled to have made his ground. However, when the television replay of the action was shown, those in the hospitality boxes around the ground – most of which had TVs – began to howl their objection. South Africa's captain, Hansie Cronje, asked for the third umpire's decision. While the two standing umpires discussed the situation, Cronje and Brian McMillan approached Thorpe and appeared to suggest he should give himself out. Thorpe was having none of it. Meanwhile, the decision had been belatedly referred to the third umpire, and Thorpe had to go. Throughout the incident, the cameras focused on the players and officials, picking up the tension in and drama of the stand-off between Cronje and Thorpe. Not only had the decision come about because of Cricket TV, but the consequences were the stuff of great television.

The reality of Cricket TV is that similar situations will continually arise. It has been the case that any player expressing any dissent – whether seen by the umpire or caught by the cameras – has been disciplined (in the above instance, Cronje was fined). In one incident in Australia in 1994/5, Mike Atherton was actually off the field and half way down the players' tunnel when TV cameras caught him taking his annoyance out on a plastic chair. Cricket authorities need to arrive at a sensible arrangement concerning the relationship between players, their emotions, and the television cameras. Players have been dissenting, sledging and taking it out on chairs since cricket began. The difference is that now every gesture and reaction can be seen in close-up.

The Australian Cricket Board have led the world in their acceptance of the increased role of television, embracing many of the changes Packer wished to introduce. In contrast, the English cricket authorities have been slow to appreciate the development of Cricket TV. The 1995 TCCB/BBC/BSkyB contract included the provision of a television magazine show. Shortly after the announcement of the contract, a senior source at the BBC explained how any magazine show produced by the BBC (or Sky Sports) would be subject to the approval of the cricket authorities. 'Our hands are tied by the MCC,' it was said 'We can't do anything remotely contentious because they would come down on us like a ton of bricks.' Keith MacKenzie denies that this is the case. 'I'm not aware that the TCCB have any editorial control over us – that's not how we work.'

Well, maybe. But BSkyB's coverage of the home test series in 1995 and the accompanying magazine show were so timid and deferential as to render them trivial, and the BBC's magazine show was little more than a publicity vehicle for David Gower. Whether any attempt to influence their coverage was implied or explicit, it may be enough that the broadcasters are aware of the conservatism of cricket's governing bodies. This alone could be enough to deter Cricket TV's producers, who are well aware of how much money their bosses paid for the privilege of covering cricket, from following a more adventurous course.

Cricket's higher profile has led to a considerable upping of the ante in terms of the money involved in the game. Contrary to popular opinion, there is certainly an audience for Cricket TV. The BBC's audience research shows that approaching one and a half million viewers watch test matches. That figure goes over four million at peak times (at weekends, when people are at home). With the knowledge that test cricket is a significant draw, the TCCB signed a new deal covering the TV rights for English domestic and test cricket in the summer of 1995. The deal will last four years, pointedly ending the year before the 1999 World Cup, due to be held in England. In return for a joint bid of £58 million, the BBC will continue to broadcast the test matches live, with Sky Sports broadcasting highlights for the first time. In addition, the BBC have lost the rights to live coverage of the one-day international series which will be shown live on Sky Sports, with the state-owned channel left with highlights. The domestic one-day competitions have been divided between the two broadcasters. Both the BBC and BSkyB are to produce magazine shows. At the time of the deal, there was a rumour, which the BBC did not repudiate, that they had made no attempt to bid for the one-day internationals, assuming that they would lose out to BSkyB.

Given the huge influence television has on the development of cricket, the ownership of the TV rights for the game and the question of who gets to show it are increasingly important. That the BBC didn't bother to contest the rights to the one-day games was seen at the time as a pragmatic move. Along with the story of the battle over the rights of TV coverage of the 1996 World Cup, it could well presage the future of Cricket TV.

Originally, the rights for the 1996 World Cup were bought by a consortium of British TV companies, CPP-1, eager to get a large sporting event to boost sales of their cable TV package. But the channel which was to broadcast the competition went bust and the consortium decided to sell the rights on. The only real bidders were BSkyB, who had bought the TV rights to the previous World Cup, and the BBC. Bidding was also complicated in a minor way by the fumbling advances of LiveTV, a small cable channel run by former *Sun* editor Kelvin MacKenzie. In the end, the event was bought by BSkyB at a knock-down price.

What followed was farce. The BBC had been given – according to them – a verbal undertaking that they would be allowed to show highlights of the World Cup in return for a payment of £1 million. Once the deal between BSkyB and CPP-1 was completed, however, BSkyB – according to the BBC – reneged on the deal. The BBC was left high and dry.

While this dispute was taking place, the Broadcasting Bill was progressing through the House of Lords. As a result of BSkyB's success in snapping up a number of high-profile events, politicians on all sides were baying for legislation to 'protect' a list of the UK's annual sporting highlights – including home tests, Wimbledon and the FA Cup final – from falling for the temptations of Rupert Murdoch's wallet. There quickly followed meetings between Prime Minister John Major and (separately) the BBC and BSkyB. The deal between BSkyB and the BBC reappeared and was completed the same week.

This was the second time that Major had intervened between Sky and the BBC on behalf of cricket fans. The Cricket World Cup of 1992 was, by all accounts, an exciting affair. But to those English fans without access to satellite TV, it was a non-starter. England got to the final, a not unprecedented event, but it seemed destined to be viewed by the majority of the public as a thirty-second insert on the news. Major intervened and BSkyB dutifully sold a highlights package of the final to the BBC. It should be noted that Major's likely successor as prime minister is not a cricket fan. BSkyB and other non-terrestrial broadcasters are unlikely to experience the same pressure from a football-supporting prime minister.

There is a danger that the amount of money on offer might tempt the cricket authorities to sell out to a minority channel.

The fear must be that cricket gets its own cricket-only channel on either satellite or cable. While this would have many advantages for those cricket fans who will watch anything, its effect on the game of cricket could be catastrophic. The casual viewer – the person who drops in and out of test matches, and probably watches only one-day games – will not have access to televised cricket. Without access through television, it may not be possible to draw new fans into the game. The effect will be to tighten the noose around the neck of cricket, choking off the supply of players from any source other than those, mostly public, schools which force cricket upon their pupils. We can already see the effect that this has had on the national game.

It is arguable that unless televised cricket is rammed down the throats of the public, the game in Britain will die. Perhaps the time has come for the BBC to start its own satellite sports channel. This would allow the BBC to bid for sporting events on an equal footing with other satellite companies and would enable them to guarantee highlights for terrestrial BBC. In addition, it would generate revenue for a reportedly cash-starved BBC. Though it may seem irrelevant to the game, it may well be that decisions like this define the future of cricket in England.

The expansion of Cricket TV has forced a change in the role of the other media. Radio coverage of test matches – both at home and on England tours abroad – has been the preserve of the BBC. It began in a time before television coverage of the game and grew steadily in stature and meaning. At its height, cricket fans would watch test matches on television and listen to the commentary on 'Test Match Special'. Cricket radio's job was always going to be difficult, given the development of Cricket TV; but the past five years have seen its decline become freefall. Though in many ways the poor relation of TV, radio did manage to hold down a place by providing something more than the mere reporting of the matches. John Arlott's retirement from 'Test Match Special' in 1980 could have crippled it and certainly did leave a gap. However, the death of Brian Johnston in 1994 appeared to have brought an end to the era of cricket radio as entertainment. Although Arlott had been the voice of cricket for a generation, Johnston had been its spirit. By the early 1990s he had become an anachronism in broadcasting, but the very enthusiasm and Woosterish charm that marked him out were so powerful they transcended their roots in the 1940s and 1950s and touched a later generation. But with the passing of Johnston, cricket radio lost its character. Caught – it seemed – between the lighter entertainment values Brian Johnston epitomised and the more serious tone of pundits like Christopher Martin-Jenkins. The days of watching the test on TV with the sound down and the radio up were over. Cricket radio in the mid 1990s is often little more than a dreary reportage of events on the field.

All may not be lost. The increasing use of visiting commentators and expert summarisers with some knowledge of the modern game is making 'TMS' commentary more listenable again. It's to be hoped that the producers of 'TMS' try and encourage that trend as well as studying the approach of broadcasters like Radio 5 Live's Alan Green, the football commentator who has revived the practice of simultaneously watching sport on TV and listening to the radio.

With the increased coverage of all sports on the broadcast media, the newspapers have had their reporting role undermined. Cricket news is usually reported by the broadcast media. Results and comment are instantly disseminated by radio and TV, or through the teletext services. The broadcast media has the desire and the ability to lead and create the sporting news agenda. As Keith MacKenzie from BBC TV says, 'There's nothing worse than opening the newspaper and seeing a great story that happened the day before – and that you missed – splashed across the front page.'

Rather than playing catch-up with television – a game they will always lose – newspapers have moved to define and fulfil a different role. As Rob Steen, formerly a correspondent for *Today* and now with the *Sunday Times*, points out, 'Your role as a journalist is no longer just to report what goes on.' Steen sees this as an opportunity for writers rather than correspondents to flourish:

'Its made it easier for good writers to get jobs as sports reporters and help people enjoy the game. The role of newspaper writers now is to paint a broader picture of the game, and to try to get a sense not only of the facts of the match, but also of the occasion. TV treats cricket very much as showbiz, and there's very little insight into the players.... I'll discover more of what's going on in a test match during the day [from a newspaper].'

However, newspapers have not totally surrendered the newshound's role to the broadcasters. The British press, led by its infamous tabloids, have added a significant new element to the cricket news agenda by treating it as a source of front-page scandal.

The central cricketing figure behind this increased interest in the sport by news editors was Ian Botham. His rise to glory in the late 1970s and early 1980s coincided with an era in which the expectations and importance of national teams were exaggerated. This was partly due to Britain's – or, more accurately, England's – inability to come to terms with its own mediocrity as a world power. This left sport as the only means of asserting any superiority. A deeper, and perhaps equally telling, reason was the way in which the idea of Englishness – so carefully created in the last century, nurtured by the succeeding establishment and supposedly embodied in the values of cricket – was unravelling faster than a royal marriage. The results of the England cricket team reflected the diminishing self-regard of the English. Consequently, cricket journalists – and other sports commentators – tended to lapse into a kind of hysteria. Since England's test results were generally bad, greater and greater feats of journalistic hysteria were required. Increasingly, cricket appeared to offer opportunities for those in both the tabloid and broadsheet press looking for real scandal. Inflammatory issues, such as ball tampering and accusations of racism, began to become a staple part of the coverage of a test series.

Before Botham, cricketers were generally left alone by the tabloid press. After Botham, cricket could never be free of them. As major stories go, he was, in Graham Gooch's words, 'a godsend' for the press. Loud, opinionated and a bit of a carouser, Botham provided English cricket and the national press with something they sorely lacked: a winner. Botham was both assisted and damned in achieving this status by the most unlikely ally.

The editor of the *Sun* through most of the 1980s, Kelvin MacKenzie, was obsessed with cricket. MacKenzie's amazing powers of prescience were to be called on regularly during the *Sun's* long and tortuous relationship with cricket in general and Botham in particular. Botham was signed up by the *Sun* to write a column even before his first England appearance. Following the debacle of the first test in the 1981 Ashes series, MacKenzie had a change of heart and demanded Botham's resignation, telling his sports editor, 'If you signed the cunt, you can sack the cunt'. Whether MacKenzie recanted this opinion following the heroics of Headingley, Old Trafford and Edgbaston isn't documented. The sports editor and his successors, however, ensured that Botham continued to write for the *Sun* for most of the 1980s.

After 1981, Botham became the almost exclusive property of the tabloids. Initially, they were his greatest supporters, but they didn't take long to turn on him. As early as the 1982/3 tour of Australia, with Botham's form suffering, he was pursued by the tabloids who were keen to find a reason for his decline. Tale after tale emerged in the following years about Botham's off-field life. From his admission that he had smoked cannabis (which resulted in his suspension by the TCCB) to alleged bedroom romps in Caribbean hotels, the tabloids had their teeth in Botham and they wouldn't let go.

Rob Steen saw at first hand the reaction to Botham from journalists: 'The jealousy towards Botham was quite incredible. It's so much part of this country's nature to love putting people down.' The pattern discernible in Botham's story – also known in the trade as 'build em up, knock em down' – is renewed by the press on a regular basis. Darren Gough, prematurely elevated to superstar status following his heroics against South Africa and Australia at the end of 1994, suffered at the hands of the press because of his lack of form after an injury.

During the Pakistan tour to England in 1992, the hysteria of the press turned downright distasteful.

Already smarting from England's defeat in the World Cup final the previous March, the English press was ready and waiting for the Pakistanis when they arrived. The *Cricketer*, reporting on the one-day series that preceded the tests, saw 'The lads in the tabloids...busy drumming up a nice little line in Christian/Muslim warfare which made the crusades seem like a forty-over match.' The *Daily Mirror* was already busy doing its bit for international relations, calling Javed Miandad 'Cricket's Colonel Gadaffi'. This tone remained for the duration of the fraught series.

Following an incident in the third test when Aquib Javed was warned for bouncing Devon Malcolm and then became embroiled in a dispute over a jumper with umpire Roy Palmer, the *Sunday Telegraph*, in the shape of political correspondent Simon Heffer, weighed in. Accusing Pakistani players of 'degrading' cricket by their behaviour, Heffer urged the TCCB to ban future tours involving Pakistan. The hysteria reached a crescendo after the series when Allan Lamb, writing in the *Daily Mirror*, accused the Pakistanis of ball-tampering. Though disciplined by the TCCB for breach of contract (players are not permitted to give interviews or write articles or books without TCCB authorisation), Scyld Berry, writing in *Wisden*, described popular opinion as largely in favour of Lamb. However, Berry qualifies his statement by pointing out that this was probably only for finding an excuse for England 'staging four spectacular collapses and thereby losing the series'. Lamb and the *Mirror* were sued for libel by Sarfraz Nawaz, who, Lamb claimed, had 'shown him an old trick...a dozen years ago'. In the end, the case was settled with neither side able to claim victory, despite the caravan of English crick-eters prepared to wind their way through the High Court to aid Lamb and the *Mirror*. The following autumn, the *Sunday Telegraph* apologised to 'the Board of Cricket Control for Pakistan, to players and to all Pakistani cricket followers' for Simon Heffer's article.

Part of the reason for the development of this hysterical media coverage is that the Conspiracy of the Press Box is alive and well all over the world. Though claiming that conspiracy is far too strong a word, Rob Steen does admit that there is a strangely close relationship between papers who in most areas are fiercely competitive. 'All the tabloid cricket correspondents have assistants who do most of the leg work. What happens at five o'clock in the afternoon is that they all get together and ask "What's the line today? Who are we going to talk to?" An agreed tone is reached.' Steen puts this approach down to the the 'paranoia and lack of security among tabloid journalists'. This 'paranoia' applies not just to cricket, Steen points out, 'but to any major sport where you know your story is going to be on the back page'.

As someone who has known these pressures, Steen is keen not to dismiss them. The world of cricket correspondents is by definition very small. While in England, they tend to congregate for test matches, spending their time between the press box and any television or radio work they can get. There are not very many major cricket journalists, and those that there are know each other intimately.

The past ten years have seen the number of people in press boxes swelled by the introduction of ex-players as the main source of comment and analysis, not just within the press, but within the sports media generally. Their ability to comment from personal experience and their expert knowledge of the circumstances of playing the game are now considered prerequisites for the presentation of sports in the media. Channel 9 in Australia has a strict 'ex-players only' policy regarding match commentary, and a similar policy is pursued by BBC TV. The desire to take a more player-centred approach to cricket writing has led to a change not just in the journalists, but also in the way cricket is covered. Personal knowledge (i.e., of players and playing) now has a higher value in media terms than historical perspective. 'Knowledge of the history of the game is very slim among correspondents, let alone the audience,' says Rob Steen.

There is one other aspect of the game in which the print media continues to play a major role. Although television has been the driving force behind cricket's modernisation, it is the newspapers – especially the broadsheets – that usually lobby for changes within the game. 'Newspapers have a completely different function in terms of cricket than in terms of sport generally,' says Rob Steen. 'Television leads the way up to a certain point, but when it comes to getting things changed, newspapers have a lot more clout.'

The new roles of the cricket media, although gradually becoming apparent, were thrown into sharp focus during the first test between England and South Africa in July 1994. The Mike Atherton ball-tampering affair helped redefine both the respective roles of the cricket media and the cricket establishment's attitude to that media. Involving an incident which may well have passed unnoticed without TV cameras, a (predictably) hysterical reaction from the press and, eventually, a career crisis for a radio correspondent, all of the features of the new cricket media came to the fore.

At 2.45pm on Saturday, 23 July 1994, the BBC broadcast pictures of Mike Atherton removing dirt from his trouser pocket and applying it to the ball. Atherton was caught not once, but twice, performing what Tony Lewis (commentating on BBC TV) called 'the Aladdin's Lamp treatment'. The BBC producer, Keith MacKenzie, was director at the time of the incident.

'All we were doing was showing and reporting what we saw,' says MacKenzie. 'We don't get into a situation – particularly with a live game – of necessarily getting stuck into somebody. We're not judge and jury; we're there to show what has happened. We can comment, and the commentators are there for that reason. When you get a controversial incident like that, the people who tend to make the most out of it are the press.'

MacKenzie understates the case somewhat. The papers went ballistic. Many writers in the broadsheets and tabloids accused Atherton, either directly or by implication, of cheating. Others were equally as fierce in his defence. The *Mail* (along with assorted correspondents in other papers) supported Atherton, expressing the view that 'had he been raised by a couple of lesbians and attended some terrorised secondary modern' he would have been lionised.

The events of the Atherton affair illustrate the new relationship between the media and cricket. That ball tampering was a major issue was beyond doubt: the stakes had been raised in 1992 and thereafter by the press's attacks on the Pakistanis. But the reaction from the management of England and the TCCB demonstrated their determination to take on the media. This they did, essentially by learning from the political practice of the day. The Atherton case coincided with a rash of government ministers being found to have behaved in various reprehensible ways. Atherton, Illingworth (the England chairman of selectors) and the TCCB – with more success than the Government – decided to front it out. Unlike his predecessor, Ted Dexter, Illingworth took what appeared to be definitive action – Atherton was fined – and toughed it out (when in trouble, Dexter famously made pronouncements on facial hair and Indian smog).

A feature of the debate that followed was the reduced role played by the established cricket press. Though they commented freely, and usually in Atherton's favour, it made no difference whatsoever. Things were rumbling on a far deeper level. The *Times* opined in a leader that, 'if the captain of England's cricket team fails to uphold the values of his society...he should be replaced.' In Atherton, it seemed, the drama of the destruction of that most bizarre of constructs, 'Englishness', was played out. It appeared that Atherton was to take the rap for all those government ministers who didn't. Everybody was keen to have their say. Atherton himself remembers calls for his resignation from 'the Headmasters

Conference...and fucking Jimmy Tarbuck! I thought that was the day I had to resign, when Jimmy Tarbuck told me to go!'

Finally, the media acquiesced, by turning on themselves. The BBC's cricket correspondent, Jonathan Agnew, expressed the view that Atherton should resign. What followed Agnew's call was the questioning of his own position. Writing in the *Independent*, Mark Lawson said Agnew should be the one to go, essentially because he had put the weight of the BBC behind calls for Atherton's dismissal. Matthew Engel, for the *Guardian*, asked whether there was a difference between Agnew calling for Atherton's resignation and the hypothetical situation of Robin Oakley (the BBC's political editor) demanding John Major's head. Michael Parkinson, interviewing a tired Agnew for the *Telegraph* (he said he hadn't slept for three nights), felt that Agnew had 'underestimated the responsibilities which went with the prefix BBC'.

Agnew survived, as did Atherton, but both remain keen not to have the subject brought up again. That the debate moved on to this territory served two purposes: it helped save Atherton's neck by diverting attention from him; and it gave the press someone to vent their spleen upon. What probably finally saved Atherton was that he had no real competition for the job at that time. The net effect of the Atherton affair is that since 1994 the cricket media has been loathe to attack the England captain. While the team continued to be ridiculed, Atherton's persistence and personal good form with the bat ensured his survival. It was not until the tour of South Africa in 1995/6 that a combination of bad results and poor team management put him under pressure once more.

It is a truth universally acknowledged that an England cricketer in possession of ability must be in want of charisma. Cricketers from other countries appear not to have this problem. Since the early 1990s, cricket has seen the devel-

opment of a new breed of superstar. There are now three cricketers – Shane Warne, Brian Lara and Sachin Tendulkar – who
are easily recognised in every cricket-playing country by
millions including those who are not interested in the game.
They have achieved this status, through a process not unlike
that which creates pop stars, largely because of the media.

In the same way that pop music creates and needs stars in
order to continue, so does cricket and the cricket media.
English cricket has had no real stars since Botham. In Botham
we see the ideal example of the way the media and cricket feed
off each other. Botham, obviously a man with a lot to say,
wants to say it to a lot of people. Throughout his career, he
bemoaned the intrusion of the tabloid press into his life; yet he
was also pleased to take their money (by writing for them),
their adulation and their company. Yet it is partly as a result of
the press's treatment of Botham that younger players are loath
to tramp down that same path.

Despite this, the media's interest in cricket can only be a good
thing. Cricket is competing with other, more glamorous sports
for the attention (and money) of the British public. The
Australian experience shows that there is much to be gained
from the press and television coverage, one-day games and
other paraphernalia of modern cricket. Cricket TV hasn't
stopped the Australians rising to become the pre-eminent test
team on the planet. As television's influence on the game
becomes all encompassing, perhaps we can look forward to the
first day/night international matches in England sometime in
the next century.

There is a widely held view that cricket is a pre-industrial
game, ideally played by the good local folk on the village green.
It may well be that in swathes of middle England this is still the
case. But for the rest of the world, cricket is a modern, post-
industrial game played for big money in front of huge baying

crowds and – essentially – huge television audiences. Graham Allen, a Labour MP and cricket lover, is fond of saying that Packer and World Series Cricket saw cricket's transition from feudalism to capitalism. To continue the metaphor, the last few years have seen cricket's transition to the information age. Rather than seeing cricket as a throw-back to the past, Cricket TV makes cricket the first twenty-first century sport.

'Cricket 2000' is how Australian batsman Ian Davis described the 1977 WSC Supertest series. Davis may have been a bit premature, but from the heightened TV coverage to the hysterical press, from the third umpire to day/night cricket, the media is now the message. What Packer sowed in 1976, every cricket fan reaps. Cricket 2000 est arivé.

HEROES OF THE REVOLUTION

10

THE UNEASY FIGUREHEAD: MATTHEW ENGEL

Matthew Engel's impact on the creation of the New Cricket Culture cannot be underestimated. He was the first to write about the game in a language and style that made it seem part of the late twentieth century. He also, with his coverage of the South African debate during most of the 1980s, played a major part in challenging the partial and divisive view of cricket's place in the world that had grown to dominate the game over the last century.

It is a laurel that sits uneasily on the diffident Engel's head. Indeed, it must have seemed like a crown of thorns during the debate over the right of foreign-born cricketers to play for England during the summer of 1995. Many of his admirers were shocked when he did not condemn out of hand an article in *Wisden Cricket Monthly* that many regarded as racist.

There would have been a New Cricket Culture without Engel. But like Marqusee, Engel significantly added to its intellectual weight and moral force. And like *Sticky Wicket*, he also helped shape its language and attitude.

Here he is on Ian Botham breaking the world record for the number of test wickets.

Play had started late, the opening overs had proceeded peacefully enough, it was time for a bowling change. Up trots

Botham. His loosener was intended as such, hardly more than a log hop. But Bruce Edgar, transfixed by the legend more than the ball, or perhaps just anxious to play a bit-part in history, waved his bat and helped it to second slip. The crowd erupted. Botham erupted, made a series of gestures that indicated he was quite pleased with himself and embraced Gatting as though they were long-lost twin brothers, which in a way they are. Amid the scrum of players Gooch asked: 'Who writes your bloody script then?' If it comes from a comic strip, it is from a new one: Ian of the Clichés or the Wizard of Ego.

Botham came into this match with a post-comeback bowling average of 131.5. For pointless hours in Antigua, Botham bowled and bowled in an attempt to get that wicket. Now one suspension (for admitting to smoking cannabis), four months and a million column inches later he had done it at the first attempt. Don't ask for a cricketing explanation: there is none. We are into the paranormal.

When that was written in 1986, and certainly by now, people had become used to this approach to cricket writing. Martin Johnson began his career at the *Independent* displaying all the style of Engel, if less of the political nous, and today the papers are full of Engel-copyists. But back in the early 1980s, when Engel started writing for the *Guardian*, his arrival for many was the equivalent of hearing Elvis Costello for the first time. Costello was doing nothing strange, there were plenty singer-songwriters obsessed with the same subjects. But none sounded as urgent and relevant as Costello. And Engel's writing was and is no different.

Engel was born in 1951 and grew up in Northamptonshire. He spent much of the 1960s packing his duffel bag with banana sandwiches and setting off to watch Colin Milburn and

Mushtaq Mohammad try to transcend Northants's mid-table mediocrity.

During these days out, the young Engel would often see the man with 'the best job in the world', the cricket correspondent of the *Northampton Chronicle and Echo*. Years later, when Engel arrived at the *NC&E*, a fresh-faced graduate, that same correspondent was winding down and considering a move into teaching. Within weeks Engel had his dream job. Engel remembers that his enthusiasm for the job was not discouraged by the man he replaced. 'He was particularly delighted I wanted to do the Sunday league'.

The *NC&E* during the 1970s was often produced in a state of chaos. This lack of organisation allowed Engel the freedom to break most of the staid conventions of local newspaper sports reporting. 'I am sure that on a more conventional and better-run local paper they would just have beaten the shit out of me and told me that "you don't do it like that"', he says. Instead, his bosses went along with his freewheeling style, even encouraging it in an idiosyncratic way.

'I started putting jokes into the very first sports report that I did. The deputy sports editor, a dotty old boy, liked them so much that he kept putting exclamation marks after them to show how funny he thought they were. I had to very politely talk him out of it, and although he couldn't quite understand why I was upset he reluctantly agreed.'

Engel eventually left the only job he thought he'd ever want to do, driven mad by the *NC&E's* disorganisation. He spent two years with the Reuters news agency before getting a job as a sports sub-editor on the *Guardian* in 1979, after the sports editor mistook him for somebody else. In an uncanny echo of his experience at the *NC&E*, Engel discovered that *Guardian* cricket correspondent Paul Fitzpatrick had decided to concentrate on Rugby League, and there was an unexpected vacancy for one of the most prestigious jobs in cricket journalism. 'There were loads of people mad keen on football, who all desperately wanted to be David Lacey, but for some reason no one on the sport's desk wanted to report cricket', Engel remembers.

Engel was offered the chance to follow in the footsteps of Cardus and Arlott; when he appeared to hesitate, the editor declared that Engel 'could bloody well edit the paper then and let him report the cricket'. But finally Engel accepted, admitting that it was a job he would have 'killed somebody vaguely unpleasant to get'. He remained the *Guardian's* cricket correspondent until the 1987 World Cup, before falling victim to 'world-weariness' induced by five consecutive summer and winter seasons. He became a general features writer who was still involved with the paper's cricket coverage, but 'not every day, not all day, not any more'.

As the *Guardian's* cricket correspondent, Engel found a curious mixture of inertia and tolerance at the paper. 'There were one or two very gifted people in senior positions who let you do things in ways that other newspapers, certainly at that time, would never have allowed. In the early eighties there was no *Independent* and the *Times* and *Telegraph* were moribund. The *Guardian* in many ways was a very bad paper, but it got away with it because there was nothing else. If you had any spark at all, you read the *Guardian*. I just wrote in a way that felt natural to me and assumed that if a joke or reference to something happening outside the game appealed to me, then it would probably appeal to the reader.'

Engel was pretty much known only to *Guardian* readers until the announcement, in 1982, of the first rebel tour to South Africa. Here was a story which, because of his interest in and feel for political issues, Engel alone of the cricket correspondents was willing and able to tackle properly.

This is what he had to say about a day/night match between South Africa and the Australian rebel party that toured the strife-torn country in 1985:

The crowd was as near to all-white as you could get in any country south of Iceland without actually barring the gate to blacks. This was due partly to sporting taste, partly to geography. The Wanderers ground is in the heart of the amazingly affluent northern suburbs, where public transport is a rumour and the blacks are second-bottom of the social scale, some way ahead of the car-less.

The crowd was not quite the largest of the week in these parts. Forty thousand had gathered the previous day in the township of Mamelodi to hear Winnie Mandela talk of vengeance at a mass funeral of blacks killed in the unrest. The police kept a low profile there too, though for different reasons. Except for the odd journalist, it seems improbable that anyone was present at both events or knew anything, beyond the haziest outline, of the other.

At the Wanderers, when the supper-time rain eased off, smoke canisters were lit as part of a sky-diving display. That is the nearest Kim Hughes (the Australian captain) and Co are likely to get to tear gas as they continue their love affair with the bright, shining, hospitable face of this country. Hidden away is a different South Africa, which the cricketers believe exists in the imaginations of foreign journalists. Good care is being taken to ensure that they never see it, hear about it, or think of it.

Engel followed the story of the South African rebel tours from its beginning to its tragicomic end, covering visits by the unofficial West Indian team, as well as those by English and Australian players. He soon became known to the South

African cricket establishment as 'the leader of the opposition'. 'South Africa wasn't a matter of enormous complexity as far as I was concerned', says Engel. 'It was very obvious to me who was right and who was wrong and I knew that the good guys had to win.'

Engel's opposition to the tours may have been in tune with popular opinion in the UK, but it put him in a very small minority as far as the cricket world was concerned.

'I once told a county cricketer that I thought there were only six people on the county circuit who would refuse to go to South Africa as a matter of principle, rather than simply refusing to go because they could make more money playing test cricket. He said, 'Well I'd bloody well go if anybody asked me' and I thought 'Oh shit, that means there's only five'.

Engel is perfectly aware that there is racism in the cricket world as, unfortunately, there is in other aspects of British life. He was once told by an English cricket official that Pakistan's objection to umpire David Constant standing during the 1987 test match series was rejected because 'we couldn't let the fuckers get away with it'. He was left in little doubt that if the request had come from Australia it would have been complied with immediately and without question.

However, he does not believe that the cricket world's support for South Africa was based mainly on racism.

'Cricket is such a time-consuming game that people who are involved in it often imagine that it is all there is. I think that is what happened to some players, writers and administrators over South Africa. They weren't sufficiently in touch with anything else to see the whole picture.'

Not that Engel minded being out on a limb; in fact, he appears to have rather enjoyed it.

'To some extent, I was on the edge. I was in South Africa, at the height of the anti-apartheid campaign, writing antigovernment stuff. There was always the sense that I was under some kind of threat, although perhaps I fancied myself in more danger than I actually was. For the most part, I was treated with elaborate courtesy by the South African cricket authorities. However, there were occasionally nasty moments with sporting, and sometimes civil, authorities.'

The beauty of Engel's reporting on South Africa was that while he maintained a resolutely anti-apartheid stance, he also retained a sense of proportion about the whole affair and never resorted to the 'blood-spitting' of many opposed to the rebel tours. He realised that major forces for change in South Africa were always going to be political and economic; and, while he supported the sporting boycott, he always acknowledged that – should apartheid end – South Africa would have much to contribute to international cricket.

His approach also allowed him to take a level-headed approach to the effect of the rebel tours on the English game. While most of the English cricket press were tearing their hair over the 1989 rebel tour led by Mike Gatting. Engel saw it instead as the perfect opportunity to dispose of 'players with a past, but no future'. The English test team had just suffered the worst period in its history, winning just one game, against Sri Lanka, and losing ten out of the last twenty-four. Engel suggested that the loss of underachievers like Neil Foster and John Emburey would force the England selectors to give younger players a chance. Over the next year players like Alec Stewart, Angus Fraser and Mike Atherton all cemented their places in the test side and England secured eight victories in the following twenty-four games.

Finally, Engel's understanding of the political situation in South Africa always meant that he remained relatively optimistic about the possibility of change. While politically naive cricket commentators preached apocalyptic visions of a split between black and white cricketing nations over South Africa, Engel understood how quickly political change could make such talk a nonsense. In the end the change happened even faster than Engel expected, which is no surprise given that most full-time political commentators were shocked by how quickly apartheid was defeated.

But if Engel was an angel in the eyes of anti-racism campaigners over South Africa, many thought him the very devil when the row over foreign-born players representing England exploded in the summer of 1995. The trigger was Robert Henderson's article in *Wisden Cricket Monthly*. The piece started controversially enough, suggesting that the selection of test players in most countries was 'racially determined'. But the real source of controversy was his questioning whether black or Asian players born and raised in the UK feel 'the same pride and identification with the place as a white man'. Henderson then claimed 'It is difficult to see how playing for England could be anything more than a means of personal advancement and achievement for players of West Indian ancestry.... All the England players I describe as foreigners [i.e., anybody not white or raised in the UK] may well be trying at a conscious level, but is that desire to succeed instinctive, a matter of biology?'

Henderson had been circulating the article for some time, trying to find a publisher. I even received an unsolicited copy of the unpublished article after Henderson mistakenly concluded that my book on overseas players, which he had not read, supported his own offensive views. Eventually the article was picked up by *Wisden Cricket Monthly*, whose editor David Frith was a man of strong right-wing views who consistently supported the renewal of sporting links with South Africa and was never averse to a bit of liberal baiting.

On publication, the article attracted blanket coverage in the national media. Both Phillip DeFreitas and Devon Malcolm sued and secured substantial damages, while the magazine was widely censured and forced to print an apology.

Engel, much to his irritation, was dragged away from working on the book he was writing to respond to the article for two reasons: firstly because Henderson had cited Engel as a supporter of his views; second, and more significantly, because Engel was a long-time member of *WCM's* editorial board. Engel by this time had also been appointed editor of the *Wisden Cricket Almanack*, which was owned, along with *WCM*, by multi-millionaire John Paul Getty.

Engel's response to the article, which was printed in the *Guardian*, had all the hallmarks of a reaction from somebody whose mind was elsewhere. He chose to tackle Henderson's two main points, dismissing the 'biology' argument as 'drivel', but agreeing that patriotism did often boost sporting performance. He believed, with some reason, that his views on racism were widely enough known not to have to address the issue directly. Unfortunately, he was wrong.

Engel's views on the issue have been consistently maintained over a long period of time. He told a meeting of the Cricket Society in January 1988: 'I'm utterly opposed to the circumstances under which people born overseas can play for England. There is a very clear distinction between who is genuine in this matter and who isn't. People who came to England to play county cricket and who wouldn't have come to England if they were not offered a contact by a county club shouldn't be allowed to play for England. I think that Hick playing for England is outrageous'.

Today he says: 'My views are very clear, or anyway they're clear to me. I most certainly do not believe that there should be any racial discrimination in the English cricket team or anything else. I do believe that the qualification rules to play cricket for England are too lax and that there is a possibility that some of the people who have played for England for a number of years may have chosen to regard themselves as English, not out of patriotism, but because it was the only way they could make a living as cricketers. This could have damaged the English team'.

He adds: 'I was in a difficult situation over Henderson. I felt that my overriding duty was to defend the name of *Wisden* as best I could. Whether I would now, knowing the extent to which my views would be twisted, I'm not sure. I think I was badly misinterpreted. I will accept a portion of the blame, but I think part of it was wilful misinterpretation. I'm resentful that anybody thinks I've changed my views.'

Like most writers, Engel has difficulty analysing his own style. He modestly refuses to believe that he was doing a better job than other, more experienced cricket correspondents, but he does admit that his perception of the game when he began writing might have been 'fresher'.

He says that he is only a modest reader of the game, lacking the ability and desire to watch every ball in the way that allowed the former *Times* cricket correspondent John Woodcock to be so authoritative. 'I had to work like crazy just to keep up,' he claims.

But Engel had one great advantage over any other full-time cricket writer, alive or dead, and it emerges in a chance remark about South Africa: 'I was unusual in that although I was opposed to the South African regime, I was riveted by its efforts to survive. This came down to the ambivalence that I have always had between being a sports writer and a political writer. The story was made for me, I was fascinated by it. I am always fascinated whenever sport moves into the real world. That's what really interests me.'

Engel's approach obviously gave him a huge advantage when

dealing with issues like South Africa, but it also gave him an understanding of human nature that writers who were obsessed with the game's minutiae lacked: 'Because I'm able to see the game in a political way, I can often see fairly clearly how things will develop. For instance, when the England manager Ray Illingworth said before the 1995/6 tour to South Africa that he would be the only selector, I was able to point out that this would not happen. There are politics in any situation and the dynamics of a tour are such that you can't pick the team without consulting the captain.'

However, the other side of Engel's broad world view is not to overdo 'the cricket as a metaphor for society' approach so beloved by some writers who wouldn't know the real world if it came up and bit them in the arse.

'Although it is important to write about the game in the context of what is going on around it, it's important to remember that cricket is only a game. 'It's an enjoyable, worthwhile game and it is worth trying to understand it properly in all its beauty and complexity. But it is not the only thing in life. I was always determined to uphold the tradition of *Guardian* cricket writing created by Cardus and Arlott, and not taking the game too seriously is a big part of it. The joy of cricket comes when it is part, not the whole, of life.

'There are only about five hundred people in this country who are involved in the game full-time. The huge majority of people who are interested in the game have lives beyond cricket. They don't watch all day every day, in fact they're very lucky if they can have a day at the cricket at all. If there's a test match going on, they'll be vaguely conscious of it, moving in and out of contact with it whenever they get access to the radio, TV or newspaper. That's how most people follow the game and I have always been very conscious of that being the kind of person I am writing for. We may share many of the same reference points, but they aren't necessarily obsessed with cricket, it's just part of their life.'

Many have wondered how this approach gels with Engel's appointment to the senior position within cricket journalism, the editorship of the *Wisden Almanack*.

Engel argues that he now has 'a different role to play', claiming that editing *Wisden* imposes all sorts of responsibilities and restraints on any journalist.

'The *Guardian* was always going to survive whatever I did as cricket correspondent. To me the tradition of Wisden and how I handle it is very important. I have to ensure that I am able to pass on that tradition. To ensure that Wisden is there forever and continues to remain a fundamental part of cricket.'

Engel also points out that when he writes the editor's notes each year, he is writing 'for a hundred years' time, for posterity'.

'Last year I decided I was going to have to be critical of Illingworth's approach to the England manager's job. I felt very strongly that he was doing things the wrong way and I knew that I couldn't bottle out of saying it. And I also knew I was going to have to say it between hard covers in a book that people were likely to take notice of and would probably be reading in a hundred years' time. It's a hell of a difference from writing a piece that is going to be wrapping chips the next day.

'I went through agonies; I had sleepless nights. I lay awake at 3am with the wording going round my head over and over again. Eventually I came up with a form of words that expressed what I honestly thought in what I hoped was a responsible and fair-minded way. And I know that it was infinitely more effective and influential in the debate than anything I ever said about Peter May (England's highly unsuccessful chairman of selectors during the 1980s) in the *Guardian*.'

But hasn't being appointed editor of *Wisden* caused Engel to lose his radical edge?

'I have never been radical about cricket', he claims. 'Radical is when you want to change something fundamentally. I do want some aspects of the game to change, but basically I want it to go on as before. You can't be truly radical about cricket and still love it. The two are contradictory. What you can do though is bring radical perceptions to bear on your love of cricket.'

Engel is 'no great believer in changing the structure of the game'. It is a case, he says, of everybody having 'a plan that will not work'. He would like county cricket to have the same kind of impact as the Football League, but knows that that is highly unlikely. He also suggests that the tensions between domestic and international cricket and between one-day cricket ('fundamentally uninteresting') and the first-class game ('a wonderful, rich, complex, lovely game') are mostly 'unresolvable', largely because of non-cricketing pressures.

He claims that there is 'no one answer' to cricket's problems and that all the game can do is try and 'steer carefully between traditionalism and modernism, without going to one extreme or another'. The one specific idea he does mention is the introduction of a world test match championship, which he claims would have 'an enormous impact on the game in places where test cricket is suffering'.

Engel also thinks that if England found two fast bowlers who stayed fit most of the talk about the need for a two-divisional championship and a cricket academy would soon dry up. 'The first reference to the fact that the game was not what it was and that we were unlikely to see such giants again was in 1854. There's always someone, somewhere, who's sure the game is in crisis,' he says.

Engel has a typically pragmatic view of the bodies that run

the English game. He points out that the Test and County Cricket Board is in theory 'a very democratic organisation', with county members able to exercise direct influence on the TCCB through their clubs. However, he acknowledges that 'inertia' is always likely to prevent any major change.

He also claims that it is a 'fundamental weakness' of English cricket that the MCC, 'a private club whose appeal is essentially snobbish and social', is the 'richest and, in many ways, the most important force in the game'. Ideally, he would like the money that the MCC membership generates 'to be channelled into something more democratic'. However, he also believes that the MCC has 'enormous strengths and that its conservatism has been one of them'. In many ways, he claims, 'it has been a judicious steward of the game'.

So is the responsible, non-radical Engel now part of cricket's establishment?

'I see Wisden having three traditions: integrity, accuracy and independence. Integrity is the most important, but independence is not that far behind. The fact is that Wisden has never been part of the establishment and has never been tied to the official view of the game. I hope that Wisden always retains an authoritative, independent and sometimes troublesome voice, because that plays an absolutely central role in the game, as well as being vital to the Almanack's success.'

But hasn't *Wisden* usually pushed the ideas the establishment would like to promote but knows it lacks the public support for? Did not Engel's predecessor Graeme Wright write a book immediately after relinquishing the editorship suggesting that the MCC should regain control of the game? Doesn't Wisden simply serve the same purpose as the *Spectator* does for the Conservative Party?

'Not on my watch' is Engel's answer.

11

THE INSPIRATION: MIKE MARQUSEE

In Mike Marqusee's kitchen there is a photograph of his father sharing a joke with Martin Luther King Jr. It is an arresting picture, the great black leader and the middle-class white guy obviously at ease in each other's company. It emanates a feeling of trust and commitment. Both of Marqusee's parents were heavily involved in liberal politics and he grew up surrounded by countless examples of what it takes to commit yourself to a cause that doesn't directly affect you, but has right on its side.

Marqusee was soon protesting against injustice himself. At the age of twelve he took to the streets of Scarsdale, the affluent but soulless New York suburb where he grew up during the 1960s, to join in the counter-cultural revolution. He claims his parents put no pressure on him to take an interest in politics and that the decision 'to get involved' was all his own. Very soon the right-wing Legion of America was trying to run him out of town for supporting the legalisation of cannabis; his enthusiasm for that particular cause was as much influenced by the desire to 'hang around with Lou Reed' – busy changing the face of popular music in nearby Manhattan – as by a passion for civil rights.

'Politically and culturally, the sixties completely shaped my life and the way I look at everything', says Marqusee. 'I was fifteen in 1968 and I followed every aspect of the student revolutions around the world, like I now follow a test match. I knew which side I wanted to win. I was completely partisan and I still am.'

By 1971 Marqusee was weary from the struggle and headed for the supposed pastoral delights of southern England and Brighton-based Sussex University. He has lived in England ever since and has become heavily involved in left-wing British politics, eventually writing a book detailing the failure of the Kinnock's Labour Party and supporting the efforts of his partner, Liz Davies, to secure a parliamentary seat despite the objections of Tony Blair and the Labour Party modernisers.

All of which has everything and nothing to do with Marqusee's success in writing the finest book on cricket's role in society since C.L.R. James's *Beyond a Boundary* and providing an intellectual focus for the New Cricket Culture.

Although Marqusee's political background informs much of what he wrote in *Anyone But England*, reviewers' obsession with the fact that he was an 'American, Marxist cricket writer' obscured much of the universal power of his argument. What Marqusee did was to deconstruct the old-fashioned and one-dimensional view of the game that dominated cricket (in England at least), and reveal the possibility of a much more democratic and diverse future for the game. It is an achievement that this book tries to build on.

As it did to *Sticky Wicket* editor Peter Hardy, the cultural hijacking that has afflicted the game since the turn of the century became obvious to Marqusee during the debate over the rebel tours to South Africa.

'We were constantly told that all cricket fans wanted to see England play South Africa,' claims Marqusee, 'and that all this worry about apartheid was imposed from outside the game. The reality was that, while the cricket establishment desperately wanted links with South Africa, most fans thought the idea was crap and had nothing but contempt for the Gooch and Gatting rebels. These fans lived in the real world, knew that sporting links with apartheid were unacceptable and didn't want to see cricket blemished in that way. And yet you had people like former *Times* cricket correspondent John Woodcock and others wanting to renew links with South Africa and claiming to speak for the cricket world. But it was plain that they only spoke for a tiny bit of it.

'It was assumed that if you were a cricket fan you had this reactionary, prejudiced, public-school world view. But that's never really been true. It's just that most cricket fans have never had their voices recognised.'

Because the minority view of the game's culture has held sway for so long, many in the UK had come to treat it as gospel. But the way in which Marqusee came to the game allowed him to see through this accepted wisdom.

'I didn't encounter cricket until my early twenties and this gave me the advantage of not having had it forced down my throat when I was a kid. To begin with it was a form of escapism from the intensity of my life between the ages of thirteen and twenty-three. I liked baseball, and cricket was like baseball, only more so. It was even slower, even longer, even more ritualised and even more complex, which was what made it stimulating and satisfying. But although I chose cricket, I never did so consciously. I just went to a few games and got chatting to people, particularly West Indian friends who had their own particular way of looking at the game. Things that seemed natural to people who had grown up with it raised questions to me. I also had a different sporting and social culture, which I could compare cricket to. I had absolutely nothing invested in the traditional hierarchical English cricket culture. It seemed like a complete joke to me from the beginning. My first reaction to learning that they wouldn't let women into the Lord's pavilion was to enjoy the absurdity of it, although I soon began to take that sort of thing more seriously.'

Marqusee's grass-roots education took place in Somerset during the mid seventies. This was a strangely cosmopolitan time, with acid casualties selling dope behind the pavilion and enjoying the county's first taste of success along with the agricultural workers who made up the bulk of the county's fans. On the field the young Viv Richards was bringing black power in every sense to southwest England, while Brian Close was transforming Somerset from a group of entertaining make weights into a disciplined, modern cricket team.

This cricketing education mirrored Marqusee's political rite of passage and gave him a view of the game robust enough to withstand the 'little England' nonsense pedalled by most commentators.

'I don't think that cricket is English. I don't presume that the cricket culture that people here grew up with is intrinsic to the game. Two years after I first saw cricket in England, I was watching it in India. I soon realised that cricket doesn't belong to any particular culture. A guy with dreadlocks and a spliff seems to me as much to do with cricket as an MCC member with his striped tie and G & T.

'There have always been many cricket cultures and those that try and narrow it down to one, who always claim to be the defenders of some inner purity, are the enemies of the game.

'When the signs of major upheaval in the cricket world arrived with the Packer circus, cricket's establishment couldn't deal with it because they lived in a world that was utterly stagnant and decaying. The First World War had shattered the Victorian view of the game for the intelligentsia and for the working class, but the aristocrats and middlebrow administrators still lived in this dream world.'

And for all the talk of change, Marqusee says that those at the top of English cricket are still stuck in the same old mind-set. 'They are just as unaccountable, just as fixated with money and just as dedicated to aggrandising the top of the hierarchy as those that they succeeded, largely because they are the same type of people.

'Researching *Anyone But England* I was amazed to find just how unchanging the hierarchy of the game is. People forget that when the Test and County Cricket Board was created in the late sixties, it was supposed to be a modernising, accountable body, whose creation marked a break with the domination of the MCC. Yet just look at who is currently chairman of the TCCB – D.R.W. Silk, a public-school headmaster and former president of the MCC. If he's not the old school tie then nobody is, yet he's supposed to be the spearhead of modernisation.

'There has been little change in the nature of the people running English cricket over the last fifty years. It is still a mixture of financiers, businessmen – especially from booze and tobacco companies – former civil servants and military men. The only influx during recent times has been the media and PR people from today's celebrity culture. But they've changed things very little. Even supposed rebels like Mick Jagger want nothing more than to sit in the Long Room wearing their egg and bacon ties and pretending to be one of cricket's old guard.'

But Marqusee warns against getting too caught up in what he calls 'the phony war between modernisers and traditionalists'. For example, he dislikes the coloured clothing which goes with one-day contests – on aesthetic rather than nostalgic grounds – but welcomes the introduction of the third umpire – not because it is a 'modern' idea, but because it rewards good fielding, one of cricket's most important skills. 'The much more important issue is whether the game is being run democratically and its wealth fairly spread around,' he says.

Marqusee's research for *Anyone But England* revealed to him that cricket's multiculturalism has a long history.

'Michael Foot [the former Labour leader] put me onto the extensive cricket coverage that the Socialist newspaper the *Clarion* gave to cricket before the turn of the century, and it's clear from the writing of C.L.R. James that there was a distinct West Indian cricket culture then.'

Marqusee says that this multiculturalism is now finally making itself felt because England's decline in international cricket has weakened the stranglehold the old school had on the game. 'No one takes the establishment men of English cricket seriously now. How could you? Even by their own standards they are failures.'

Marqusee claims that the vacuum left by the establishment's failure to produce a winning English side or to revive the fortunes of the county championship has allowed the New Cricket Culture space to grow. He also believes that sport in general is gaining an even greater importance in people's lives, claiming that it is now 'bigger than pop music'.

'True, people might not be turning up to watch cricket as they once did,' he concedes, 'modern life doesn't often allow such a luxury. But they follow it with equal passion through the media. This renewed interest in sport, including cricket, has created a "consumer rights" movement which is shaking up much of the game's received wisdom, such as why the game stops every time there's a little rain or the sun goes behind a cloud.

'The grass-roots revolt has already happened in football and now it's happening in cricket and rugby union. It has been more traumatic for cricket and rugby because they have rigid, top-heavy governing structures and ideologies. There was less of a battle in football, because the people who ran the game did so as a business and had few pretensions towards being some kind of moral guardians. '

It is a pretension that is easily dismissed by Marqusee. He points out, for example, that one-day cricket (which the old school claim to detest) was introduced not because of some great clamour from the unwashed masses, but because those who ran the game wanted an easy way to raise more money.

'It's often claimed that limited-overs cricket owes its subsequent popularity to the fact that the majority of modern sports lovers are too thick to enjoy the longer form of the game,' says Marqusee. 'The allegation is that all of us out there under the influence of television have short attention spans, vulgar tastes and only like instant gratification. This is just ludicrous snobbery and it is based on the most fuddy-duddy view of popular culture. Aspects of popular culture, like the New Cricket Culture, are not entirely spontaneous, but neither are they completely manufactured. They are a reaction between commercial and grass-roots pressure, and as such can be just as challenging and complex as high culture.

'Take fielding for example. The standard of ground fielding has gone through the roof, largely thanks to one-day cricket. But admiring this is regarded as a somewhat vulgar pleasure, despite the fact that a good throw from the boundary on the turn is just as skilful and dramatic as a cover drive.

'The real reason behind the rise of one-day cricket is that most casual followers of the game can only afford to spend a handful of days watching cricket each season. Because of this socio-economic pressure, the temptation will always be to go and see a match in which you are guaranteed to see all twenty-two players and a result.

'Changing the structure of the game will have little impact on the decline in popularity of first-class cricket and the growth of the limited-overs format. Only a significant shift in how society forces people to divide their lives between working, family and leisure will accomplish that. But still there is significant pressure to instigate a kind of perverse deprivation theory on the followers of the one-day game. "If we play less one-day cricket," the theory goes, "people will come to watch the three-day game instead." It's ridiculous. Most just won't come at all.'

Marqusee's multicultural approach to the game does not mean that he believes partisanship has no place in a cricket-lover's heart.

'Partisanship is an essential part of any game, particularly any team game. I think a lot of people unfairly misinterpreted *Anyone But England* as some sort of denunciation of anybody who supported England. Supporting one team and wanting them to win enriches the whole experience of watching cricket.

'One of the real beauties of modern professional spectator sport is the love/hate relationship you can have with a team: it's a kind of human comedy. It becomes a display of these huge emotions which, when they're played out in personal life, are completely traumatic, or in politics are very grave, and puts them in a place where they are totally harmless and probably very good for you. The idea of loyalty to a losing side is beautiful. In a society where success and personal advancement at the expense of everything else are worshipped, institutionalised and encouraged, that kind of hopeless love is really touching.

'But I think there is too much nationalism in the world today and because, unlike most football, big cricket matches are played between nations, I think people in the cricket world have to tone down the nationalism. I love the banter and the barbed comments of rival supporters, but on a national level it takes on other meanings and burdens.'

According to Marqusee, it is important to remember that people usually choose which football or county cricket team to support quite by chance. When people swear allegiance to a nationality – which in practice usually means backing a government or a cause – they do so (or should do so) because it embodies a value system of which they approve. Sporting choices are made on irrational and emotive bases and are largely governed by the accident of birth. 'That is why,' says Marqusee, 'contrary to what George Orwell said, sport has nothing in common with war. I'd like to see people choosing which test side to support in the same arbitrary way they might decide to support Manchester United if they were born and lived in Suffolk.'

Marqusee has come under considerable criticism for holding this view, the runner Kris Akabusi once memorably laying into him for this 'academic' approach to the game. But Marqusee believes that he is just reflecting the increasing cultural mix of most societies. 'I know that I am in the minority, but people like me, who have lived in more than one country and culture, are getting much more numerous.'

Marqusee is at pains to point out that using a person's support for a cricket team as some sort of political test is not just associated with those on the right.

'I was asked to speak to a meeting of the Socialist Workers Party', remembers Marqusee. 'It was packed out, showing just how much interest there is in cricket on the left. After I'd finished talking, one guy got up and said that it was the SWP's "revolutionary duty" to support anybody who was playing against England. He added that Socialists should cheer every time a West Indian fast bowler hits an English batsman. I think this makes them as guilty as "the other side". They have turned which test team people support into a political issue; it's the Tebbitt Test in reverse.'

Marqusee believes that the whole debate around cricket and nationality, which has blown up over the last ten years, is closely associated with England's shrinking role in the world and the paranoia this has created. He dismisses the cliché that the English are good losers, contrasting the English soul-searching with the positive outlook taken by the Australians.

'When the Australian cricket team went through a bad patch in the mid eighties, sports fans just became interested in tennis and rugby and waited for things to right themselves. What that reflects is that Australians are relatively sanguine about the future of their country and their place in it.

'If the English team lose you'll have people like Ian Botham appearing on TV moaning that the British people are uncomfortable with success. This is utter, self-serving garbage. The fact is that England were the most successful country in sport, politics and commerce for well over a century and that just isn't possible anymore. The constant comparison between then and now means that everything is viewed in negative terms and the focus is on losing.'

According to Marqusee, the future of English cricket should not only be about learning to win more – with the strength of most of the younger test-playing nations growing every day this is always going to be hard to achieve – it should also be about being able to lose without getting hysterical about it. Marqusee surely speaks for millions when he says: 'Whenever I hear Botham or Mark Nicholas moaning about England's latest thrashing, I think, "If that's how you feel then do another job". I watch cricket for fun, as do most people, and I think the commentators and players should remember that. We don't want to see Mike Atherton slouching around the field with a sour look on his face. He's a lucky man to play cricket for a living and he should cheer up.'

Marqusee was pleasantly surprised by the mainly positive reviews of *Anyone But England*. The *Cricketer's* E.W. Swanton groaned that Marqusee had 'a warped intelligence', but Marqusee was used to much worse.

'My first book, *Defeat from the Jaws of Victory*, which was about the failure of the Labour Party to win the 1992 election, was reviewed with unbelievable hostility. My experience in the Labour Party during the 1980s and 1990s is that alternative views are not only not wanted, but that the people who voice them are considered sub-human. For all its conservatism, hideboundness and blimpish silliness, the cricket world is actually more diverse and more open than today's Labour Party.'

Cricket has always had room for the harmless eccentric and Marqusee was treated with courtesy by people in the cricket establishment who would have had apoplexy if they had been asked to endorse his views. However, this soon changed when Marqusee became involved in the Hit Racism for Six campaign, which was launched in response to an article in *Wisden Cricket Monthly* claiming that black players were unable to demonstrate the same commitment as white colleagues when playing for England. 'When I was an individual nobody took me seriously; once I became part of a group things started to get really hostile,' says Marqusee ruefully.

Hit Racism for Six was virtually ignored by the cricket media, with the honourable exception of *Johnny Miller 96 Not Out*. One cricket writer, who had praised *Anyone But England*, was moved to describe Marqusee as 'an untrustworthy shit' because of his involvement in the campaign. In hindsight, Marqusee says that he should have seen this backlash coming.

'The single longest section in *Anyone But England* covers the 1992 ball-tampering affair. I don't say that the Pakistanis were innocent, just that they were the victims of double standards and that the coverage of the whole affair was riddled with racist stereotypes. With the exception of the Asian press, not one reviewer mentioned this section. It was OK for me to write about it, but no one was prepared to engage in the debate.

'Once we decided to debate the issue of racism publicly by launching Hit Racism for Six, we just got dumped on. We were accused of being politically correct, of imposing values from outside the game and of using the issue of racism as a cover to push our own politically motivated agenda.

'But this is total rubbish. Racism is a reality in the game and anyone who examines the game's recent history must conclude that. Devon Malcolm told us that if he signed the declaration supporting Hit Racism for Six he'd never be picked for England again.'

Marqusee says that the episode in which Malcolm was censured for his remarks during the 1995/6 tour of South Africa was another example of the way the cricket media refuses to address the issue of race.

English cricket manager Ray Illingworth decided, along with bowling coach Peter Lever, that Malcolm's action needed to be altered. When experiments at the start of the tour failed to do this, Malcolm was publicly denounced by Lever who called him a 'cricketing non-entity'.

After returning home from the tour, Malcolm slammed into the English management and was quoted as wondering whether he would have received the same treatment had he been white. Malcolm was widely attacked for his remarks and had to issue a statement through his solicitors stating that he did not intend to suggest any racism on behalf of the English management.

Marqusee was enraged by the whole affair.

'It is a classic case of blaming the victim. Devon Malcolm, despite all the pressure on him not to say otherwise, finally admits the possibility that racism might have something to do with the way in which he was treated. And he's blamed for bringing race into the matter.

'The whole affair smacked of putting the black man in his place. Malcolm arrived in South Africa on a clear high. He had just won substantial libel damages from *Wisden Cricket Monthly* over the Henderson article, despite being advised by David Graveney, secretary of the Professional Cricketers' Association, selector and manager of the last rebel tour to South Africa, not to bring the action. He was lionised in the townships and greeted by Nelson Mandela, the most famous and admired individual in the world, with the words, "So you are the destroyer". There were obviously plenty of people involved in English cricket who were clearly unhappy with the attention Malcolm was getting.

'The people who introduced racism into the game were the racists. The trouble is that issues like this force you to take sides. The suggestion that Hit Racism for Six introduced race into the game is a self-serving lie from those who want to preserve the integrity of their own little sporting oasis. We just wanted the game to be untainted by racism. We've tried to be moderate and constructive, to raise people's awareness of the problem. We know the situation won't improve by people ignoring it.'

There is a pragmatic side to Marqusee's anti-racism. He sees in Britain's ethnic communities a great interest in the game, which could significantly add to English cricket's wealth and playing strength.

This touches on what is perhaps Marqusee's greatest fear, that cricket is in danger of becoming a game watched and played only by a shrinking group of white, middle- and upper-class males. For this reason he is against 'elitist' approaches to encouraging talent like the Australian cricket academy. He is equally disturbed by the high ratio of first-class cricketers whose family have links to the game or who attended public school. 'This smacks of both favouritism and a lack of choice in young talent,' he says.

Marqusee believes that England should follow the South African example and produce a wide-ranging development programme that would give kids of all backgrounds access to high-class coaching. This should be financed by cash from the TV deals, very little of which is finding its way to the game's grass roots he claims.

Challenged on the left's perceived hostility to competitive sport, he eagerly takes the chance to puncture another of cricket's myths. He acknowledges that there is a 'puritanical' tendency held by some people with-left wing views to believe that sport is some sort of capitalist conspiracy, taking the place of religion as the masses' opium, but dismisses that view as laughable.

He says that the Labour Party activists have made considerable efforts to keep the game alive in the UK.

'It was the Tories who forced councils to sell off their playing fields and make huge cuts in their sports and leisure budgets. They also introduced the National Curriculum, which placed such a workload on teachers that they didn't have time to get involved in after-school activities like cricket coaching.

'In contrast, it was the "loony left" – people like MPs Jeremy Corbyn and Bernie Grant – that helped set up the first state-run cricket college at Haringey. The college has now become another victim of the Tory cuts, but while it was going it helped provide a focus for the huge interest in the game in the West Indian community of northeast London.'

Another left winger, Chris Searle, helped found the Devon Malcolm Cricket School at a Sheffield comprehensive. Searle, a close friend of Marqusee, had previously been the educational advisor to Maurice Bishop, the Marxist leader of Grenada. According to Marqusee, Bishop had planned to make Grenada a new centre for test cricket in the Caribbean, before the US invasion put paid to all his plans.

Marqusee is unsure whether the New Cricket Culture in all its guises will achieve a prominence in the game. He is sure, however, that if it doesn't many people will become disillusioned with cricket. The likeliest result, he believes, is that part of the NCC will get co-opted by the establishment, in the same way that major US record companies tried to exploit Gangsta Rap. In that case, of course, companies like Warner found that they had bitten of more than they could chew.

And with that Marqusee ends our conversation. Grinning, he says he has to write a letter of complaint to Islington Council. 'They've marked out a baseball diamond in Highbury Fields, the traitors.'

12

THE PIONEER: PETER HARDY

It was no contest really. Who would you rather idolise, Elvis Presley or Trevor Bailey?

Until the arrival of rock and roll, most teenagers had sportsmen as heroes. But once pop music took centre stage, sports stars became gods with feet of clay. For thirty years, pop music moved with enormous speed, constantly reflecting the desires and concerns of the people who loved it. Sport, especially cricket, appeared out of touch in comparison.

Between 1955 and 1985 the music explosion popularised rock and roll, rockabilly, doo wop, rhythm and blues, soul, country and western, the blues, psychedelia, modern jazz, prog rock, heavy metal, reggae, ska, funk, disco, punk, jazz funk, hip hop and countless other styles. Faced with this huge variety and energy, sport seemed tired and old-fashioned. If you were hip, you weren't into sport.

There was only one exception. Football always enjoyed some measure of hipness. This was partly because the sheer size of the sport made it an inescapable part of popular culture and partly because many long-haired, working-class footballers looked and acted like pop stars. But cricket? Forget it.

Those cricket lovers that were into pop music, as well as other fashionable aspects of popular culture such as the cinema, knew it was best to keep quiet about their interest.

Cricket, it seemed, could only be enjoyed in a way that had changed little since the 1950s. The introduction of one-day cricket, day/night matches, the Packer revolution and the South Africa boycott all showed that cricket was being affected by the modern world, but in the commentary box, committee room and pavilion you wouldn't have been surprised to hear people wondering when rationing would end.

And then, in April 1988, *Sticky Wicket* arrived.

True, there had been signs that things were changing. Matthew Engel was obviously writing for people born after 1950 and Ian Botham's 1981 antics had given the game its first national hero since Denis Compton. But *Sticky Wicket* took things to a whole new level. Finally the modern generation of cricket enthusiasts had decided to follow football's example and have their say about the game they loved.

Sticky Wicket followed in the footsteps of football fanzines like *When Saturday Comes*. In his book *Fever Pitch*, Nick Hornby claims that *WSC* and the rest of the football fanzine movement gave the game new hope in the wake of Heysel and other hooligan-inspired tragedies. Cricket, thankfully, faced nothing so terrible, but it did have to cope with the long decline of its popularity and relevance. *Sticky Wicket* helped reverse both, although the extent of its impact is unlikely to become obvious for years to come.

Sticky Wicket was so influential for two reasons. First, it covered the game in an irreverent, politicised and entertaining way that was much more in tune with the last quarter of the twentieth century; and second, it proved the inspiration for other members of the New Cricket Culture to produce their own fanzines. Hard on its heels followed *The Cricketer's Anorak*, *Whose Surrey Now*, *Over and Out*, *The Googly*, *The Name of the Rose* and the longest running and most successful of all *Johnny Miller 96 Not Out*. The New Cricket Culture even entered the mainstream with the glossy, but short-lived, *Third Man* and the arrival of *Inside Edge*.

In the wake of the fanzine explosion, the first edition of *Sticky Wicket* appears to be nothing out of the ordinary. But in eight years much has changed, and the first issue of *Sticky Wicket* was quite a shock to most cricket fans.

The cover of the first issue was stark and uncompromising, featuring a cartoon of three giant black-hooded figures – one carrying an axe, the second a rope and the third a cricket ball. The figures were superimposed on a photocopied picture of Lord's and the strap line announced the 'Return of the Executioners'. Inside, the figures were revealed to be Patrick Patterson, Malcolm Marshall and Courtney Walsh.

The *Cricketer* and *Wisden Cricket Monthly* also introduced the 1988 West Indian touring party on their covers, but neither were able to do with *Sticky Wicket's* directness and impact. The accompanying article on page three dismissed the ill-founded optimism created by England's success in getting to the World Cup final during the winter and described the home team's chances with a pessimism that was entirely justified by the series's four-nil result.

The editorial, written by *Sticky Wicket* founder and editor, Peter Hardy outlined the aims of the magazine. 'No pretentiousness will be tolerated,' he declared: 'What we need is people specialising in deadpan humour, cricket trivia and a feel for the game. Armchair supporters, daily watchers at all levels and pub knowalls please apply. If you either play or watch this great game and get as frustrated with the TCCB, Mike Gatting, Ian Botham and the pathetic activities of our national team as we do, then you are the people that we want involved.'

Hardy continued: 'It seems impossible to get the sort of witty, laconic articles that we want printed in any of the mainstream cricket press.' He called for contributions with 'a suitable blend of information and entertainment' and warned that 'extreme bias will not be tolerated, nor will pious patriotism. Rationality and detached views from around the world will.'

The first issue of *Sticky Wicket* featured a number of articles that were to become regular features during the magazine's two-year life.

The spoof 'Deloyttes Ratings' began by comparing TV commentators, with Tom Graveney being given high marks for 'suburban gentility', Ray Illingworth being marked down for his inability to say 'that' and Bob Willis receiving plaudits for his 'ironic dress sense'.

The Coaching Clinic featured Mike Gatting apparently talking us through his reverse sweep that lost England the 1987 World Cup final. The first 'Medallion Man' was Chris Broad, whose chest furniture reminded *Sticky Wicket* of 'Spanish beaches, Europop singles and shades that reflect'.

But the high point of the first issue was a parody of David Gower's monthly diary piece in *Wisden Cricket Monthly* which was soon christened 'Lubo's Filo'. In the first entry we learn of Lubo's fondness for pop duo 'Pepsi & Shirley' and hippie soft-rockers 'Supertramp', as well as his trip to see *Phantom of the Opera* by the Leicester Amateur Dramatic Society.

On cricket, Lubo records his reappointment as captain of Leicestershire and muses: 'Poor Old Will (Peter Willey). What with his knees and some of the young upstarts causing trouble, I was waiting for him to fall off his perch. Now all it needs is Gat (Mike Gatting) to make an even bigger fool of himself and I shall be a national hero again.'

The 'Filo's' depiction of the disaster-prone playing careers and culturally challenged social lives of Lubo and his England team-mates appeared frighteningly accurate. This, together with the fact that the writer's identity was a closely guarded secret, meant that 'Lubo's Filo' was soon considered required reading in the county dressing rooms.

David Gower's fiancée, Vicki Stewart, was just one of those who took out a subscription to *SW* in order to find out what Lubo, who funnily enough had a girlfriend called Vicki, got up to. The fact that her twelve-year relationship with Gower ended around the same time as *SW's* last issue is surely a coincidence.

Typical of the paranoia that 'Lubo's Filo' created in the game's mainstream was David Frith's reaction to a piece in the penultimate 'Lubo's Filo'. The *Wisden Cricket Monthly* editor took exception to Lubo describing Frith's 'pathological hatred' for then *Cricketer* editor and BBC cricket correspondent Christopher Martin-Jenkins.

Frith wrote to Hardy insisting on a printed apology. In his covering letter Frith claimed that *Guardian* writer Matthew Engel was the author of 'Lubo's Filo'. This was odd, considering that Engel was a member of *WCM's* editorial board.

Hardy printed both the apology and the letter. He also added a note pointing out that 'Lubo's Filo' was written by a tall, curly-haired, left-handed batsman, a description that could equally apply to both Hardy and Leicestershire's finest player.

Interestingly, in his suggested apology, Frith said that the other comments attributed to him were 'near the mark'. Considering that those comments included a description of CMJ as 'reactionary, boring and a prat', perhaps 'pathological' wasn't an exaggeration after all.

Despite the quality of its writing and Phillip Imber's cartoons, *SW* was still definitely a fanzine. The layout was courtesy of photocopied paste-ups and spelling mistakes and poor editing abounded. This was unavoidable as Hardy had to do most of the production work on the magazine himself.

Hardy had long wanted to produce his own cricket magazine. Like many he found both *WCM* and the *Cricketer* 'professional' but uninspired. He also disliked their covert, and often overt, support of South African cricket and the rebel tourists. But most of all he was fed up with the unwillingness to address most of the issues that mattered to the game's future.

'People like CMJ seemed to be trying to promote cricket as an ideal game without any faults at all. He has the ability to sit on the fence more than any other person I've ever come across. There never seemed to be any attempt to get to the bottom of stories A classic case was 'Alan Lee's County Cricket Diary' in the *Cricketer*. He used to skirt around subjects, because he could never bear to offend anyone. The whole impression was of a cosy little club, which would say things by implication, but never tell us what we want to hear.

'I launched *SW* in my late twenties, so I had my feet enough on the ground to know I wasn't likely to start influencing what the TCCB did. But I knew there was a lot of useful information floating around that never got printed. Most of all, I thought writing about cricket should be entertaining. People shouldn't be afraid to stick the knife in, where it's justified, and give it a little twist. I wanted to produce a modern magazine with a sense of irony.'

Hardy was determined to produce a magazine that would reflect how change in the world outside was affecting cricket and people's perceptions of cricket. He, like Engel, realised that most people didn't think about cricket in isolation from the rest of their lives. He also knew that many cricket followers usually treated the game and its participants with cynicism and irony, without loving it or them any less. Finally, Hardy wanted *Sticky Wicket* to 'revel' in the language of cricket – not the stilted tones of the established commentators, but the vibrant and ever-changing terrace slang in which you could commiserate with someone for 'having a bit of a 'mare' or damn them for 'playing like a prat'. This approach meant that *Sticky*

Wicket could address issues like crowd behaviour, coloured clothing and the rash of advertising logos that began to cover the grounds and players' clothing in the late 1980s in a way which was a million miles from the pompous pontificating or school-boy humour of the established cricket mags.

Hardy hated sentiment and refused to waste space wallowing in some supposedly glorious past. Everything in *Sticky Wicket* had to be relevant to people's day-to-day experience of following cricket in the 1980s and 1990s. Nor were there pseudo-interviews in which monosyllabic players spouted their banal opinions. Let them play the game; Hardy's men (and women) would describe their feats and sketch their characters with much more eloquence.

Hardy rejects the idea that *Sticky Wicket* was alternative in the counter-culture sense. 'Our writers held the same irreverent but relevant views as the average punter. I always wanted *Sticky Wicket* to be a mainstream magazine, one with well balanced views and a cutting edge.'

In the mid 1980s, Hardy was living in Scotland and playing for a Perth-based club. He began producing a regular club magazine and this convinced him that he had the skills and know-how necessary to launch *Sticky Wicket*. The idea became a reality when he moved down to work in London during 1987. Here, he had ready access to printers and specialist book shops, most notably the newly opened Sportspages on London's Charing Cross Road, through which to distribute the magazine.

It was, in Hardy's words, 'a low-risk venture', each issue of the magazine costing only a few hundred pounds to produce. An advert in *WCM* soon attracted not only cartoonist and layout artist Imber, but a core team of writers prepared to work for next to nothing.

Just as Hardy, a director at one of the UK's leading

recruitment firms, is not exactly the stereotypical fanzine editor, so the mainstays of *SW* were not the spotty adolescents many imagined them to be. All were hugely enthusiastic and knowledgeable about the game, they came from all over the country and most of them would never see thirty again. More than anything, they proved that for a number of years a growing section of English cricket lovers had come to feel that the mainstream cricket press had little to offer them.

Contributors to early issues included Ian Adshead (a.k.a. Horace Sledge) a high-class club cricketer and former Labour Parliamentary candidate. Blessed with a wide range of contacts and an acid wit, the Lancastrian Adshead was the cricketing brain of *SW*. A typical Sledge comment (on England's selection policies of the 1980s) was 'The England team is a bit like a WH Smith book club – it is easier to join than to leave.' Adshead also gave the magazine its name.

Another member of the editorial team was Philip Conford, an English teacher and a regular writer for the *Times Literary Supplement*. Among his contributions to *Sticky Wicket* was a savage piss-take of that blandest of commentators, Tom Graveney:

SW: Welcome to the magazine, Tom.

TG: It's very,very nice to be here.

SW: Tom, we'd just like you to listen to some brief extracts from your end of session evaluations of play.

Recorded voice – TG: Yes, it's been a very, very interesting morning indeed . . . he's played some absolutely beautiful off drives . . . marvellous . . .

SW: Tom, would you accept that those remarks are fairly typical of your expert opinion?

TG: Yes, I would say that they were very typical indeed.

SW: And would you agree that it's probable that the average fourth-former with an interest in the game would be capable of offering remarks of at least equal profundity.

TG: I should say that it's very, very probable.

SW: Then don't you feel it's scandalous that your record as an elegant exponent of the cover drive should entitle you to purvey such banality every summer?

TG: I'd say it's marvellous. A marvellous, marvellous fee.

Conford's pop at Graveney was part of a long running SW campaign aimed at highlighting the poor standard of the 1950s mafia that dominated BBC commentary teams. Most cricket fans had become fed up with the self-congratulatory tone and the lack of constructive criticism which characterised most commentaries. They were also sick of being talked down to by those who seemed to take it for granted that people wanted to hear their views, but who didn't realise that knowledge of the game was useless to a commentator who didn't have the wit to express it. SW was always widely read in media circles, and the fact that commentary teams are now (in most cases) more professional, articulate and knowledgeable about the modern game shows that although the magazine might not have influenced the TCCB, it could make the BBC sit up and take notice.

Hardy never looked down his nose at the anorak element of cricket's fan base, recognising that a love of the game's ephemara is a fine thing. The needs of such readers were met by Jonathan Bruce – the Prince of Trivia – who served up statistical gems in a pithy, unstuffy manner. Not for him the meaningless lists of firsts and bests. He much preferred the telling snapshot, such as his comment in the June 1989 issue that no England batsman had been stumped for thirty-seven tests. Bruce is, according to SW, 'a lover of all things American, ranging from the New York Yankees to R 'n' B', something you expect could not be said of Bill Frindall'.

One thing all the *SW* team shared was a strong dislike of the mediocre nature of many county cricketers. The mainstream press moaned in an ambiguous way about the lack of variety in the game, while at the same time writing trite profiles of the very players whose 'sameness' created the problem. *SW* did what the mainstream mags were afraid to do and named the guilty men.

SW took great delight in exposing the 'John Nobodys' of county cricket, players who even their mothers would admit had no real business earning a living from what is supposed to be a form of entertainment. The most successful part of this campaign was the regular series on 'trendy medium pace trundlers'. Some form of revenge for hours spent watching bowling that was best suited to Sunday beer matches was exacted as the likes of John Carr, Ian Greig, Martin Weston and even the post-1988 Ian Botham were held up to ridicule.

Unlike the other cricket magazines, whose myopic view of the world blew cricketer's problems out of proportion, *SW* also had little time for the player's whingeing. 'These guys were being paid to play the game we loved and yet they used to go on about being some sort of hard-pressed minority. One of the worst offenders was Jonathan Agnew, but I haven't heard him mention a word about it since he jumped over the fence to become a media pundit', says Hardy.

However, *SW's* real ire was reserved for the hypocritical nature of the players who would spend half their time moaning that nobody had any pride in playing for their country any more and the other half angling for a place on one of the lucrative rebel tours to South Africa. Hardy and the rest of the *SW* team were contemptuous of the players who would put spurious concerns over winter-time employment above the struggle against apartheid. As the October 1990 edition commented, it was understandable that Paul Jarvis should want to pay off his £60,000 mortgage...but in one go?

SW was also the only magazine to identify the fact that the BBC was employing a commentary team of which at least seven members – CMJ, Trevor Bailey, Tony Lewis, Jack Bannister, Fred Trueman, Ray Illingworth and Brian Johnston – spent much of the summer of 1989 giving varying degrees of support to the breaking of the sporting boycott of South Africa.

Hardy remembers how he listened with mounting depression to the ramblings of the 'Test Match Special' team. 'That sort of bias alone was a good enough reason to make sure that those with a different point of view had a chance to express it', he says.

Yet another target was the late Peter May, then chairman of the England selection committee. Hardy saw May as the perfect example of how English cricket had failed to move with the times. 'No company would be led by someone who had no day-to-day involvement with the business. May worked five days a week with Willis Faber and probably never went out of the home counties in the summer. He was supposedly in charge of the English cricket team: it was an absolute joke. Many of his decisions, like the one to pick his godson Chris Cowdrey as England captain, were tailor-made for ridicule.

'Cricket is supposed to be one of our national games, yet players were having their futures decided by someone who had a full-time job and saw just twenty days of cricket a season, and most of those were test matches. You can't tamper with people's careers like that'.

His replacement Ted Dexter fared little better at the hands of *SW*: 'My dad always told me that Dexter had a concentration span of a gnat, that he was a great theorist, but awful at getting things done. I said in *SW* that he would be alright if he could concentrate on the matter in hand. But he didn't and he made a complete mess of himself very, very quickly.'

And then there was Micky Stewart: 'He came in for a lot of stick because he never watched any incident of any significance, such as when Gatting was having a go at Shakoor Rana. He got himself out of any tortuous situation he found himself in (and there were many) by just pretending not to be there.'

And then, finally, there were some of England's leading players. Players like Allan Lamb. 'Lamb talked as if his neck was on the chopping block all the time and moaned about never being able to gain any confidence. Yet he survived – he, and others, survived year after year producing mediocre scores.

'The England team of the mid and late 1980s was packed with charm-school playboys like Lamb. David Gower was the biggest playboy of all, but at least he was a decent player. It was their approach to the game which helped England underperform after the inflated series victory over Australia in 1985. The core of that team survived for a long time without any degree of scrutiny and this undermined England's performance later in the decade.'

All this was good knockabout stuff, but it was also ahead of its time in predicting the need for reform in the management of the English cricket team, reform which is only now being put in place. The arrival of *SW* meant that, as had happened post-1985, English cricket wasn't able to sink back into a fantasy world based on past glories after a couple of successful series.

Between the end of the 1985 Ashes series and the beginning of the 1988 rubber against the West Indies, England had played twenty-eight games and won just two of them. English cricket had plunged into a deep, dark hole – deeper and darker than anything it had previously experienced. *Sticky Wicket* was partly a reaction against that and, as things got even worse during 1988 and 1989, with England playing twelve more tests and winning just one, the magazine kicked up an almighty stink. It was a wake-up call for English cricket, and however bad things seem today, in the mid 1990s, they could have been a lot worse without the desire for change which *Sticky Wicket* was among the first to express in a way that made sense to modern cricket lovers.

Perversely, *Sticky Wicket* ceased publication just as English cricket was enjoying a mini-renaissance. After producing four independent issues, Hardy was contacted by a publisher called John Brown, who said he liked the magazine and wanted to publish it.

Despite Hardy's knowledge of and interest in popular culture, he had never heard of Brown. He should have, because Brown was one of the two main figures behind *Viz* magazine, the 'adult' comic that was to become the publishing miracle of the late 1980s and early 1990s. Hardy and Brown did a deal and in November 1988 *Sticky Wicket* joined the publisher responsible for bringing the world 'Johnny Fart-Pants' and 'The Fat Slags'. It was perhaps the ultimate manifestation of how *Sticky Wicket* differed from the 1950s feel and outlook of the *Cricketer* and WCM.

Sticky Wicket was published bimonthly by Brown and began to build up a decent subscription base. However, bad luck, pressure of work and hostility from the cricket establishment combined to undermine the success of the magazine. The 1988–89 winter saw England's tour to India cancelled, and, with no international cricket, the all-important casual buyer drifted off. This situation might have been recouped if Hardy, who was still holding down a full-time job, had managed to produce the magazine monthly during the summer of 1989. But this was impossible and a pathetic performance by the English team against the visiting Aussies meant that the game's profile declined even further. Sales were hit and the momentum that any new magazine needs was lost. The magazine also had to struggle against the fact that many of the club shops at the first-class county grounds refused to stock the magazine.

As a satirical magazine being published in the late 1980s, the content of *Sticky Wicket* was nothing unusual. But the English cricket establishment is never loathe to stamp on its critics when it gets the chance, and most club shops declared that *Sticky Wicket* was 'unsuitable', so a valuable source of revenue was shut off.

This indirect censorship began to work and by the start of 1990 the writing was on the wall. On 13 May the last edition of *Sticky Wicket* appeared with 'For Sale' plastered across the masthead. Unfortunately, with the economy plunging into recession, nobody was prepared to take the risk of backing the magazine and that was that. In his last editorial, Hardy thanked the readers for their support and, fittingly, signed off with a joke: 'Mike Gatting's next tour is to the Lebanon, where he will try to get Terry Waite released this time'.

A CRICKET DREAM

13

ESPERANTO, BASKETBALL AND THE RISE
OF THE FLIPPER
Matthew Loukes

It is a brave, even foolhardy, person who makes predictions. If the soothsayers of old were to be believed, we would all be flying around in airships listening to 'Test Match Special' in Esperanto, wearing indestructible clothes and sending telepathic messages to our cryogenically preserved great-great grandparents, who remember Jack Hobbs like it was yesterday.

So when I am asked what sort of future faces cricket I naturally take the foolhardy option and gave an immediate Boil-like summary. It will, I grunt, taking a firm grip on the briar with my new teeth, be basketball. This may not be as daft as it sounds. As the rather less than benign influence of the US spreads unchecked, there is a genuine concern that cricket is being usurped in the Caribbean by the lure of the bouncing orange, rather than the cherry-red, ball. Moreover, the rules of all sports in all countries are being threatened by the reported demands of the 'public' for higher scores, more thrills and spills and, of course, more advert breaks. In this instance, the 'public' is a euphemism for TV advertisers and corporate sponsors. This lunacy has not escaped cricket, and it is a concern of many that the days of five-day test matches are numbered and soon all we will have left is the pyjama game of pinch-hitting and penny-pinching bowling.

It is my contention that it is the sponsors and the cash-hungry, dependent cricket authorities that we have to fear most. I do not for a moment believe that the 'public', whoever they might be, demands to see cricket played on a ground covered in lurid painted logos advising you to save money with a load of greedy bankers in order to pay for the insurance you will need to pay for the hospital bills incurred by the heroic number of fags you have been induced to smoke by the ubiquitous advertising. Also, it is hard to find anyone who thinks that the spectacle is enhanced by the players wearing vile migraine-inducing nylon kits. And, God help us, the sunglasses. The only people outside cricket I have ever seen wearing this *sine qua non* of naffness are middle-aged men in LA Raiders warm-up jackets loading their beer guts onto the bar on a Sunday lunchtime while braying about Brands Hatch. Most cricket fans, I suspect, are more than a little embarrassed by it all.

But the demons of the future may never arrive. It is possible for things to be better and modern without being vulgar and exclusively controlled by men whose motivation is to hoard money and power. So what if the evidence points away from that optimistic conclusion? Lenin, I think, had it, 'Despair is the infantile lower order of the revolutionary XI'. We frequently demand the so-called impossible in many areas of our lives in this rather unpleasant world, and in particular we demand it in sport: Torquay and Frank Bruno to stay up, Arsenal and Sue Barker to go down. I have even believed that Richard Illingworth can spin the ball and was actually present when Geoffrey Boycott poured scorn on the racist treatment meted out to the Pakistan cricket team. We have to make more of these impossible dreams happen (especially the Durham fans among us).

It was not very long ago that you couldn't turn on the radio without hearing some misty-eyed duffer muttering that there was no variety in the modern game because spin bowling, and leg-spin in particular, was dying. One cannot but concur that this would have been awful if it had happened, but it didn't.

Modern cricket lovers have been able to marvel at the bouncing turkey-cock strut of Qadir and the zooter-suited Warne causing that wonderful look of complete stupefaction when Gatting's off stump was pegged back. They've also been able to delight in Anil Kumble and Mushtaq Mohammad mowing down clueless county batsmen, and the extraordinary contortions of Paul Adams as he shows us all how best to check your armpits for unnecessary wetness. England fans have also had plenty of opportunity to study pavilion architecture as they watch Ian Salisbury's latest delivery dispatched over long on.

The driving (well, hoicking-to-leg) point of this chapter is to show that dismissal or despair of the future is a waste of the precious time we have left before Umpire Death walks in from square leg, with the steady Bill Alley gait and peers at the pavilion clock before removing the bails for ever.

'Az any fule kno' (except perhaps Don Mosey) the society we live in and the games we play are inextricably linked together and changes can and should be made to make them better. It woud be easy to baldly state that the problems of cricket are symptomatic of the capitalist society that endures for the time being. There is no doubt that this is true, but in a cricket context it is not especially helpful.

Come the glorious day of revolution and cricket will be played by people of equal status on freely accessible public grounds; and we will all have the time to take part as the vicious chimera of paid employment is replaced by an equitable distribution of the plentiful wealth that exists on our planet.

There, that was easy to say, if less so to read. The simple mantras of the 'Card-carrying left' can be appealing, but there is a more immediate future to face. And even if that future is looking rather like an ill-tempered Allan Donald on an Essex green-top, it is the responsibility of those of us who care about the game to face it squarely and, while humming Rachmaninov, cut and drive through it to achieve a few minor victories. I had better stop this platform oratory stuff, it takes hold of one and before you know it you are intoning Blairisms about New Labour, New Cricket, A New Game for A New Britain, tough on LBW, tough on the causes of LBW.... Time for a tea interval.

THE CALL UP TO CRICKET – SIGNING ON FOR LIFE

One could be forgiven for thinking that the New Cricket Culture is something that emerged as a result of leaving the communal box in the back of one's car over the winter without sterilising it first. Certainly, claims for the NCC as some sort of widely supported sporting movement do seem a bit premature in my view.

But, but, but...empirical and anecdotal evidence suggests that maybe more people do follow cricket now than ten years ago. Crucially, these people are different from those who followed the game in the past or, perhaps more correctly, are prepared to act in a way that is different. The fact that a fanzine like *Johnny Miller 96 Not Out* was possible at all leads one to believe that there are fans out there who are no longer prepared to put up with all the reactionary tosh spouted on 'TMS' and in the pages of the more conservative (with all three Cs) newspapers and journals.

So how did this new generation of fan become interested in cricket? In my case, I have the Government to thank.

I was forced to leave school hurriedly (expelled, sadly, for having nothing in the way of a forward defensive).

Immediately, I suffered another blow when parental disapproval of a dodgy-looking top-spinner led me into a bedsit. Here some kind employee of the Department of Social Services sent me two forms to complete. There was a mauve one for dole money and an orange one for housing benefit. From that point on cricket fell into my arms with an ease that bitterly contrasted the stubborn, Athertonian refusal of anyone else to do likewise.

The first thing my new 'lifestyle option' gave me was time. Lashings of time. With ten days until the Giro could be collected and exchanged for beer, the days stretched out like Mike Gatting's athletic supporter. I needed to kill that time and, having rejected glue-sniffing, tai-chi and looking for a job, cricket was the perfect vehicle for gobbling up the dog-day afternoons.

Mornings were devoted to sleeping and strengthening the wrist for the pull shot, so our games were often day/night affairs. A bat, a tennis ball and two or three like-minded colleagues were the passport to hours of fun. Well, in my case, hours of fielding and watching the ball being hit onto surrounding roofs. This is the sort of behaviour that one is supposed to grow out of and we were often chastised by surly security guards for the heinous crime of playing in the lorry park outside Sainsbury's, which had marvellous floodlights (SCG? Pah!). 'Ain't you a bit old for this kind of thing lads' or 'You can't do that here' could be heard with depressing regularity.

So while it came late (like some other much-longed-for activities) cricket became a large part of my life. Despite this I support no county, play for no team and have never paid to see a county cricket match, nor really felt the urge to. I suspect that I am not alone and that cricket, like Rugby Union, relies more on the uncommitted test attendee than on the county regulars so charmingly described by Messrs Gibson and Blofeld. If regular absence from work and afternoons spent shouting at Jack Bannister constitute membership of the NCC than I, and a large number of metropolitan middle-class wage sufferers, am fully paid up.

The editor has just reminded me that this is supposed to be a look at the future of The Game, and not a haphazard recollection of times past. The trouble is, how can one possibly envisage a rosy (red) future for the sport while admitting that the conditions for such a future are not exactly as ripe as Peter West's head? Well, there is nothing for it but to dream. By dreams I do not mean the random collection of old rubbish that pours forth during hours of unconsciousness (an experience all too familiar to the average Glamorgan player), but an expression of hope and conviction that 'things' and, in this instance, cricket 'things' might actually get better. (The suggestion that David Ward is a cricket 'thing' has been instantly dismissed as cruel and discourteous – although undoubtedly true.)

DREAMS OF LEG TO MIDDLING WINNING

I was in a pub a few weeks ago with a load of cricket journalists and one of them was boring for England (and the Combined Services) about celebrity cricketers: Michael 'Mike' Parkinson, Bill Wyman (whose average is yet to rise above 14); Tim Rice, Gary Lineker; Harold Pinter. At the mention of Mr Pinter I piped up in best trainspotter fashion (those who were present can judge whether I was being incredibly nerdy or just smacked oota ma coupon): 'Ah. But who is the only Nobel Prize winner to have featured in Wisden?' Sadly they all knew the answer and my hope of impressing these respected figures was dashed. 'Beckett, of course: Portora School and Trinity College Dublin.' I drifted off like Roger Harper:

Somehow off side. Nohow on side. Over. Not over. One pebble, as yet unsucked, left. All around us the field moves gently from off side to on side. It is a Sunday. It is not raining. The brief endgame. All strange away kits. We are born astride the crease. One good shout and all is over. Not over. Wide. No signals where none intended.

I drifted back. The hacks were now considering the future of The Game. An excellent opportunity to get some ideas for this task. 'Of course', one of them announced 'conjuring up a Dystopia is SO much easier than imagining a Utopia.' Fretting nervously that yet more nations had been admitted to the International Cricket Council, I fled to the snug and considered the future myself. What on earth would I really want if I had the choice? Having experienced more of the game via the media than from any physical (ahem) intercourse with it, I took the media as a place to commence the Dream.

A LOT TO BE SAID FOR ARLOTT, LESS SO FOR ALLOTT

The voice of experience has a lot to say. It knows. It has been there. It has, of course, done it. And, by golly, you are going to hear about it. As a result, one of the things I most crave in the NCC is some editorial control of players appearing in press or commentary boxes. There was a little bit of fuss fairly recently when an august member of the press suggested that some of the ex-players now writing columns were, in fact, not really very good. At first, I thought that this was another unwarranted smear on Pringer's playing abilities. But it was the quality of the writing that provoked the scribe's ire. Concern was expressed that a glut of ex-players would gobble up all the column inches of the 'quality' press, while 'proper' cricket writers were left to report on minor matches or simply ignored altogether. This does not exactly make me throw my hands up in horror, a lot of

the full-time writers have as much style as John Carr, but I think
the old geezer has a point.

Some of the ex-trundlers who could bat a bit and played with
Ian Botham are just a bit dull. Not for them the musings of
Gibson or the remarkable peregrinations of Keating. Their
prose is, well, prosaic. Prozac, even. The same applies to the TV
and radio. A huge swathe of ex-players come in and out of the
boxes and one in ten is any good. This may be a fair way of
assessing the qualities of said oldies, but is it really fair to inflict
them on me? A bit of summary, perhaps, but whoever decided
to give Jack Sinister (the Verwoerd Defensive) whole chunks of
play to chunter over needs a damn good hiding. It may be that I
am alone in holding this view and the BBC's postbag bulges
with letters of appreciation for the choices they make, but I
doubt it. Thank the Lord for Richie, his basilisk glare and
whipped delivery. I could go through the whole lot saying why
I don't like Vic Marks's giggle etc. etc., but you get the point.
Like so much of what cricket does in England, the cry is for
some selections of quality.

LOGOCENTRICITY

Why on earth do the NatWest Vultures (who are being charged
£20 for this paragraph) want their logo on the ground? Why do
Tetley think that their sales will go up if Mark Ramprakash has
their name on his jumper? Perhaps they are after the increased
consumer awareness that is generated by the TV coverage and
the pride of being associated with a successful team sport (the
sport, in this instance, rather than the team). Maybe the link
does help them a bit, but why do we have to have evidence of
this sponsorship shoved in front of our faces everywhere we
look? Does anyone who goes to the ground not know who the
sponsors are already? In the case of NatWest the bloody
competition is named after them. If cricket is able to do one

thing for me, it is to let me forget for a few overs (or until Jack is on the mike) that we have to live in a society wholly dominated by large institutions whose driving need is to make more profit. That absurd and small crumb of hope is now taken away because the fat cats are feeling just a touch peckish and as a result we must endure their logo on the ground. Why don't they take it further and put out snotty messages over the Tannoy:

Will Mr Loukes, account number 13340177, please bear in mind that the bank's patience is not inexhaustible and that the unauthorised overdraft of 17 pence incurs a charge of £800. Will the owner of car number plate MK10 7GR please remove it from the car-park because we have repossessed it due to your late payments.

And insurance. Hands up how many people have been inspired by a day's play to change their house insurance? None. I thought so. Now how many of you attended this test match as guests of some corporate sponsor or other? My God, there are a lot of you! And you make me feel sick.

Now the authorities whine that without sponsors the game would wither and die. Poppycock! The Oval could have been filled at least twice over with West Indies fans for the fifth test in 1995. Instead, they were kept out by the advance ticket sales policy and the huge number of seats given over to corporate champagne guzzlers. Even if sponsors were needed (which is arguable), why is it necessary to give in to every whim of the suits?

Horrid logo on the outfield? Of course, sir.
Vile kits? Absolutely no problem.
No tickets for black people? Splendid notion. Don't want the

sponsors' guests to feel threatened do we?
You want a 40-over thrash that knackers players and ruins technique? What, every week? How much did you say? Yes, of course.
Tongue where, sir? Yes, of course. After all The Game is the thing.

Excuse the somewhat intemperate nature of the above outburst. Contained in it (if you can see past the foam) is a weary acceptance of the fact that, given the current social conditions, some form of sponsorship is always likely to be in place. In the new world of the NCC it is a fantasy of mine that a sponsor could be found who is not greedy, demanding, vulgar and obstructive to ordinary fans' enjoyment of (not to mention participation in) The Game.

Again, I could be quite wrong (sales of England's one-day kit would seem to suggest that I am), but I want to dream of plain whites and clean fields. Now this may strike the reader as nostalgia for the good old days when Surrey and England were in their pomp and Johnny Foreigner was acutely aware of his lowly circumstance. I plead not guilty. For one, I have absolutely no idea what cricket was 'actually like' in those days, at least not to look at. My dream to do away with the current mania for logos is more a rejection of the prevailing greed than a harking-back to days of yore. Besides which (and this is as much of a motivation as any lofty political considerations) it just looks better.

WHY DON'T YOU GO AND LIVE IN ST JOHN'S WOOD
Sometimes I feel sorry for right-wingers. In the past, when confronted by a Communist, they could always summon up the response 'Why don't you go and live in bloody Russia then? Eh?' Now the poor dears don't really have that option. I

suppose some of them might mention Cuba or North Korea, but it's just not the same, is it? Another ploy used with tiresome regularity by the people who warmly agree with Woodrow Wyatt is to claim that the Extreme Left can never describe what it will be like come the glorious day. This is not really the place to go into all that (again), but the allegation does apply to the task before me.

Cricket, while not exactly a microcosm of society, obviously reflects it, and the future development of both is, as stated, linked. When there is a revolutionary change cricket is unlikely to emerge intact. For me, sitting in a dull office, with a relatively comfortable lifestyle, predictions of the future represent the height of arrogance. Worse, they imply the insulting presumption that I know what is best for the poor little workers. So I shall content myself with a few things that I, and some of the caucus of NCC revolutionaries, would like now, and hang the revolution. If that seems rather meek might I remind you of the inheritance we are promised.

First, a complete ban on players complaining about travelling. The absolute cheek of someone who gets paid (albeit not very much) to play a game, moaning about having to drive down a motorway, or (gasp of shock) get on a train, will not be permitted.

Second, spinners who do not spin the ball will be renamed something else. Spearers, perhaps, or even Richards (although that would cause a problem with rhyming slang). Spinners who can spin the ball but choose not to will be removed from our game, possibly in boxes.

Third, free access to test match tickets. A minimum number (say 25 per cent) must be on sale at the gate. This means that some poor people will be allowed in. It will annoy the racist backwoodsmen at some counties, which is a good thing.

Fourth, no more Sunday league. The collection of gate money on the Lord's day is an abomination in the eyes of God. Sorry, I got that wrong. God has been on the phone to say 'Sod the money, it is the cricket that is an abomination'. Beg his pardon.

Fifth, the immediate removal of the ban on flags and horns, etc. at test matches or, if that is going too far, a comparable ban on mobile phones, racist abuse, braying and the pish-pish noise of 'TMS' though personal stereos.

That's about it, really. No doubt there are more personal gripes and scope for improvement, I know mine change fairly regularly. For instance, at one time I spluttered with indignation at the sight of Daddles (a cartoon representative of a duck m'lud, accompanying the batsman to the pavilion on receipt of such a score). It was demeaning, undignified. Now I have grown quite fond of the little chap. Mind you, I still wince with embarrassment at Tony Grieg yelling 'Good night Charlie!' at West Indian batsmen. He, of all people, ought to have a little more sensitivity. So let this act as a taster of the sort of things that are worth getting annoyed about and those that aren't.

To the barricades comrades, and don't forget the chilly bin and the picnic, it could last five days.